The Year of the Poet X

October 2023

The Poetry Posse

inner child press, ltd.

The Poetry Posse 2023

Gail Weston Shazor

Shareef Abdur Rasheed

Teresa E. Gallion

hülya n. yılmaz

Kimberly Burnham

Tzemin Ition Tsai

Elizabeth Esguerra Castillo

Jackie Davis Allen

Joe Paire

Caroline 'Ceri' Nazareno

Ashok K. Bhargava

Alicja Maria Kuberska

Swapna Behera

Albert 'Infinite' Carrasco

Michelle Joan Barulich

Eliza Segiet

William S. Peters, Sr.

~ * ~

In order to maintain each poet's authentic voice, this volume has not undergone the scrutiny of editing. Please take time to indulge each contributor for their own creativity and aspirations to convey their uniqueness.

hülya n. yılmaz, Ph.D.
Director of Editing ~
Inner Child Press International

General Information

The Year of the Poet X
October 2023 Edition

The Poetry Posse

1st Edition : 2023

Publisher Information
1st Edition : Inner Child Press
intouch@innerchildpress.com
www.innerchildpress.com

Copyright © 2023 : The Poetry Posse

ISBN-13 : 978-1-961498-10-5 (inner child press, ltd.)

$ 12.99

WHAT WOULD LIFE BE WITHOUT A LITTLE POETRY?

Dedication

This Book is dedicated to

Humanity, Peace & Poetry

the Power of the Pen
can effectuate change!

&

The Poetry Posse

past, present & future,
our Patrons and Readers &
the Spirit of our Everlasting Muse

In the darkness of my life
I heard the music
I danced . . .
and the Light appeared
and I dance

Janet P. Caldwell

Table of Contents

Foreword   *ix*

Preface   *xiii*

Children : Difference Makers   *xv*
   Malala Yousafzai

The Poetry Posse

Gail Weston Shazor   1

Alicja Maria Kuberska   9

Jackie Davis Allen   15

Tezmin Ition Tsai   21

Shareef Abdur – Rasheed   27

Kimberly Burnham   35

Elizabeth Esguerra Castillo   41

Joe Paire   47

hülya n. yılmaz   53

Teresa E. Gallion   59

Ashok K. Bhargava   67

Caroline Nazareno-Gabis   73

Table of Contents . . . *continued*

Swapna Behera   79

Albert Carassco   87

Michelle Joan Barulich   93

Eliza Segiet   99

William S. Peters, Sr.   107

October's Featured Poets   115

CSP Shrivastava   117

Huniie Parker   123

Noreen Snyder   131

Ramkrishna Paul   139

Inner Child Press News   147

Other Anthological Works   185

Foreword
Children: Difference Makers

Malala Yousafzai

"If one man can destroy everything why can't one girl change it?" Yes, certainly a girl can change it.

She is Malala Yousafzai, the change maker from Swat District Pakistan born in July 12 1997 who changed the entire scenario of violence and gave the clarion call for peace and education.

"I truly believe the only way we can create global peace is through not only educating our minds but our hearts and our souls"

"We realize the importance of our voices only when we are silenced"

"One child, one teacher, one book, one pen can change the world"

~ Malala Yousafzai

She believed in equality. She even believed that a woman is more powerful than man. She became an international symbol of the fight for girls' education. She was shot in 2012 for opposing Taliban restrictions on female education in her home country Pakistan. She was the epitome of courage and resilience in the face of adversity

Education is one of the blessings of life that she had understood well. The United Nations officially dubbed July 12th as Malala day. She is the youngest UN messenger of Peace. she wins a Grammy Award for best children's album for the audio version of her book I AM MALALA. she was awarded Pakistan's first National Youth Peace Prize

She is the youngest person to receive a Noble Peace Prize on October 10th 2014 only at the age of 17 years. When she was only ten years old Taliban's imposed number of extreme rules. They banned girls from school. She started speaking against these strictures. At the age of 11 she worked as a blogger in BBC Urdu. She used to write the plight of the girls in Urdu when reading in seven class. She received death threats and on 9th October while she was coming from school with her friends was shot. The bullet hit her several inches away from her left eye pierced her neck and lodged her shoulder. Apparently, she was shifted to England. Various leaders condemned this.

She is an active proponent of education as a fundamental social and economic right.

"Education is neither Eastern nor western, it is human" as she said

Certainly, she is a difference maker who fought for education, peace, human rights, equality, woman empowerment and against all discriminations.

Kudos Malala; the trend setter. The whole world respects you. You are the epitome of courage.

The Inner *Child Press* with its mission of *'building bridges of cultural understanding'* takes the responsibility for global peace and harmony through poetry with International Anthologies.

We respect the land, nature, folk tales, culture, music, literature, perceptions, ideas, thoughts, language, art, artisans and all ethnic groups of the world. The year 2023 was assigned and dedicated to children change makers of the globe.

Literature has undergone a tectonic change. We express our deep reverence to all for they are the apostles of a time zone who have solved the situations, saved human lives and helped the economic, cultural social growth of society.

Malala is one among them. She is a change maker. Poetry is the living song of human race ....

"When the whole world is silent even one voice becomes powerful''. We respect the humanity. We respect the voice that speaks for justice. We admire the voice that speaks for growth of civilization.

We respect coexistence beyond any disparities.

Long live global peace ....

Swapna Behera

Cultural Ambassador
India and South East Asia
Inner Child Press International

Preface

We, **Inner Child Press International, The Year of the Poet** and **The Poetry Posse** welcome you.

We are so excited as we are now offer unto you our tenth month of our **10th** year of monthly publication of this enterprise, **The Year of the Poet**.

This particular year we have chosen to feature children who made/make a difference in enhancing the lives of all humanity. Read ~ Learn.

For those of you who are not familiar with our story, back in 2013, a few of us poets got together with the simple intention of producing a book a month. That was our challenge. Since that time the enterprise has blossomed and brought forth a fruit that seems to keep on growing as evidenced as we enter 2023.

Our purpose is simple. Through our lyrical words and verse, we not only wish to share our poetic works, but we also have the poetic naiveté to believe that we can assist in the growth of consciousness of the things that have an effect our collective humanity. Therefore, we welcome your readership. For more about what we are attempting to accomplish, have a look at our Publishing Web Site . . . www.innerchildpress.com. If you would like to know a bit more about this particular endeavor please stop by for a visit at :

www.innerchildpress.com/the-year-of-the-poet

Over the years, Inner Child Press has been socially active to bring awareness and catalog through literature the things that have an impact upon our world and its inhabitants. We have solicited, produced, underwritten and published quite a few volumes to that end. For more insight you may wish to visit : www.innerchildpress.com/the-anthology-market. If you are a writer, poet, or activist, you would be advised to keep a eye out for upcoming volumes should you desire to participate. All readers are welcomed as well. Note, that there is a myriad of published volumes that are available as a FREE PDF download as well as available for purchase at affordable prices.

We at this time extend to you our well wishes for your own personal journey and hope that you consider including us as a travel companion.

Bless Up

Bill

William S. Peters, Sr.

Publisher
Inner Child Press International
www.innerchildpress.com

Children
Difference Makers
Malala Yousafzai
October 2023

by Kimberly Burnham, Ph.D.

At 17, Malala Yousafzai became the youngest Nobel Prize laureate for her humanitarian efforts. She captured the world's attention after being shot by the Taliban in Pakistan on her way to school because she was an advocate for women pursuing education. She is currently working towards her bachelor's degree at Oxford's Lady Margaret Hall while continuing her charity work through her organization, The Malala Fund.

~ * ~

"One child, one teacher, one book, one pen can change the world." ~Malala Yousafzai

~ * ~

"I think realising that you're not alone, that you are standing with millions of your sisters around the world is vital." ~Malala Yousafzai

Poets . . .
sowing seeds in the
Conscious Garden of Life,
that those who have yet to come
may enjoy the Flowers.

Poets, Writers . . . know that we are the enchanting magicians that nourishes the seeds of dreams and thoughts . . . it is our words that entice the hearts and minds of others to believe there is something grand about the possibilities that life has to offer and our words tease it forth into action . . . for you are the Poet, the Writer to whom the Gift of Words has been entrusted . . .

~ wsp

poetry is . . .

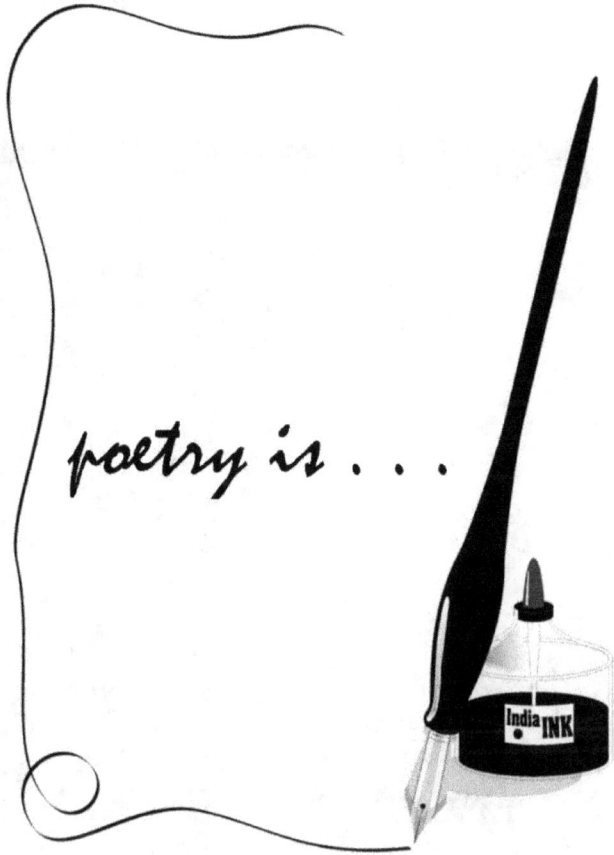

Poetry succeeds where instruction fails.

~ wsp

Now Available

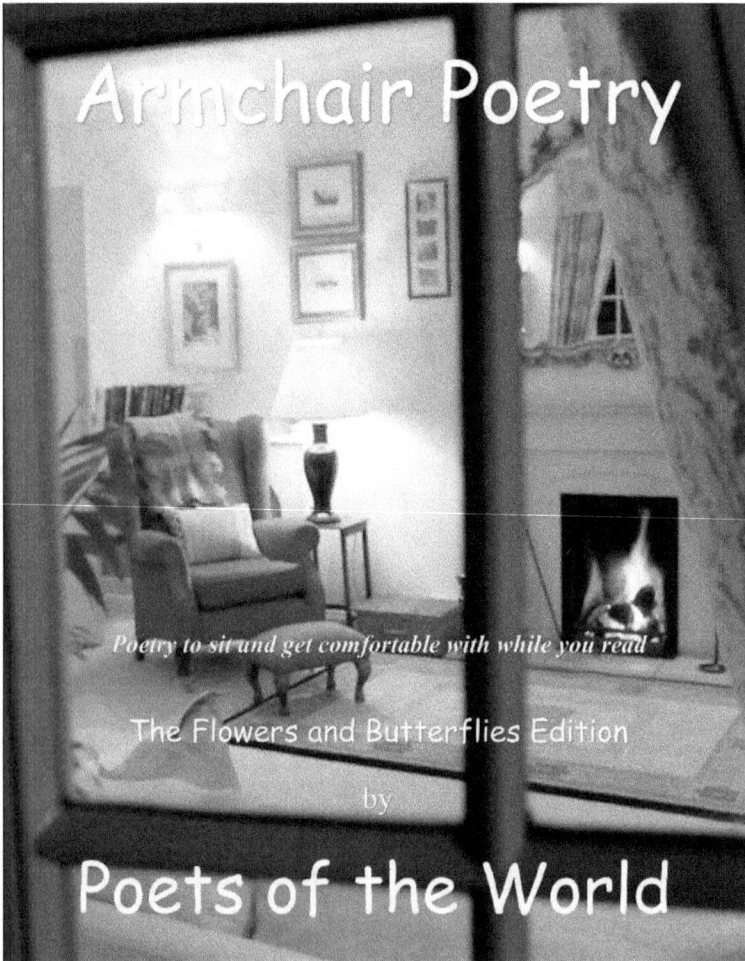

Armchair Poetry

Poetry to sit and get comfortable with while you read

The Flowers and Butterflies Edition

by

Poets of the World

innerchildpressanthologies@gmail.com

Gail Weston Shazor

Gail Weston Shazor

This is a creative promise ~ my pen will speak to and for the world. Enamored with letters and respectful of their power, I have been writing for most of my life. A mother, daughter, sister and grandmother I give what I have been given, greatfilledly.

Author of . . .

"An Overstanding of an Imperfect Love"
&
Notes from the Blue Roof

Lies My Grandfathers Told Me

available at Inner Child Press.

www.facebook.com/gailwestonshazor
www.innerchildpress.com/gail-weston-shazor
navypoet1@gmail.com

Halt

She moved slowly toward the center
Shielding the ones behind her
Her body, a barrier for ignorance
It is not that she didn't know
It was that they didn't know
What she hoped to accomplish
With the learning they thought
She really didn't need
It was never the words anyway
Life shared the space with her
The loud space we so often miss
By looking and not hearing
So they damaged her body
So they stopped her footsteps
Thinking they had won
That short pause was necessary
To gather the strength necessary
For her and her sisters

little pieces

I want to write little pieces
Very few lines with very little imagination
And even less truth
I want to live in few words
So that when I speak such
I can't be taken seriously
Because who never finishes their thoughts
Much less their sentences

I want to dangle participles
And end my angles in prepositions
Allow me to be confused also
So the world can thrive on some
Half ideas and may bees
Buzzing around on horizons
Looking through windsouls to
Free a few imaginations to soar

I need to be inconcise and unclear
Use double negatives and liberally
Sprinkle nons all over the place
Reigning drops of crowns on paupers
And use only half my wit
It will only take some consonants
And a lot of vowels, maybe all of em
To change the books that have been written

I will tell lies wholeheartedly
While I sip on lemongrass tea
I promise to be outlandish
Somewhat entertaining, but only a bit
And want things no one can do

That no one has dreamed of yet
I will drop little notes in preschools
And write snippets on playground walls
In every city's ghetto language

I will write little pieces
In very few words
With lots of spaces in between them
Room to grow child's ideas
And use crayon for lots of coloring
In or outside of lines, in or outside of rooms
Please Lord, allow my words to become less
So that someone else will have the needed
Space to change your world for the better

It's not about me

When I awake
I can lie still in the mornings
Waiting on you to join me
In that early morning grace
Of knowing that we have
Made it to today, whole,
Intact and in our right minds
I can immediately give thanks
That my prayers from
The night before have been answered
And while I may not realize it
In terms that I can touch
It never-the-less has happened

When I awake
I do not find you wanting
In any measurement of fullness
And I find your need
To begin the day in peace
A match to my own
So we go about the ministrations
A cup of tea, a heel of bread
A song of prayer, hums, whispers
Made by our own thanksgiving
Of a fast to be broken

When I awake
To the leaving and arriving
Of winds across a blue ocean
The scent of mangoes
And pleasant call of greetings
That await outside our door

It is good to be still
Against even pleasant intrusions
So we begin our day together
As we ended it the night before
In prayer for the things
We want for others and ourselves

When I wake
I am overwhelmed with
The extravagance of life
In placing me beside a man
Who understands that mercy
Is not a weakness
Nor love a fault of foolish men
But something to be treasured
And returned tenfold
When I awake
I realize that this day
Is not about me, but us.

Alicja
Maria
Kuberska

Alicja Maria Kuberska

Alicja Maria Kuberska – awarded Polish poetess, novelist, journalist, editor.

She is a member of the Polish Writers Associations in Warsaw, Poland and IWA Bogdani, Albania. She is also a member of directors' board of Soflay Literature Foundation, Our Poetry Archive (India) and Cultural Ambassador for Poland (Inner Child Press, USA)

Her poems have been published in numerous anthologies and magazines in : Poland, Czech Republic, Slovakia, Hungary,Ukraina, Belgium, Bulgaria, Albania, Spain, the UK, Italy, the USA, Canada, the UK, Argentina, Chile, Peru, Israel, Turkey, India, Uzbekistan, South Korea, Taiwan, China, Australia, South Africa, Zambia, Nigeria

She received two medals - the Nosside UNESCO Competition in Italy (2015) and European Academy of Science Arts and Letters in France (2017). Ahe also received a reward of international literary competition in Italy „ Tra le parole e 'elfinito" (2018). She was announced a poet of the 2017 year by Soflay Literature Foundation (2018).She also received : Bolesław Prus Prize Poland (2019), Culture Animator Poland (2019) and first prize Premio Internazionale di Poesia Poseidonia- Paestrum Italy (2019).

Burglary
Malala Yousafzai

who educates a boy
this one educates one human
who educates a girl
this one educates the whole world

A key made of quill pen and ink
opens the padlock to the guarded gates of paradise
The story goes that there is a tree
growing in the middle of the garden.
You can taste the fruit, open wide your eyes
to learn the rules that govern the Earth and the universe.

The lock creaks and warns that knowledge can be
dangerous
- sometimes it leads to the stake or prison,
at the same time encouraging
and saying that it is a double-edged weapon.
It is like a sword, which can cut through a veil
weaved from darkness and fear,
It is also able to destroy the Gordian knot
created from poverty and dependency.

The wide open gate invites you to get in.
The wind tries to close it and chase away the intruder.
You have to overcome your fear to break and enter,
stretch out your hand
for the bitter-tasting forbidden fruit.
Put education on one side and your life on the other.

A memory - New York, September 11th

I saw people
similar to angels without wings.
They were flying towards the ground
and they only had a few minutes to despair.
I felt my heart beating painfully.

The towers, symbols of power and glory,
collapsed with a terrible noise.
They were felled by the force of hatred

In helpless dismay
I watched history.
Then in this place
there was nothing.
The dust settled on the blood and tears.

Years have passed.
In an old chronicle
people are still jumping
from the windows.

Widow

She has been left alone,
like an expensive cup
without a saucer.

 Nobody
supports and protects her
and she cannot give
her warmth to anyone

She is still beautiful
but lonely.
She does not match the set.

Jackie

Davis

Allen

Jackie Davis Allen, otherwise known as Jacqueline D. Allen or Jackie Allen, grew up in the Cumberland Mountains of Appalachia. As the next eldest daughter of a coal miner father and a stay at home mother, she was the first in her family to attend and graduate from college. Her siblings, in their own right, are accomplished, though she is the only one, to date, that has discovered the gift of writing.

Graduating from Radford University, with a Bachelor's of Science degree in Early Education, she taught in both public and private schools. For over a decade she taught private art classes to children both in her home and at a local Art and Framing Shop where she also sold her original soft sculptured Victorian dolls and original christening gowns.

She resides in northern Virginia with her husband, taking much needed get-aways to their mountain home near the Blue Ridge Mountains, a place that evokes memories of days spent growing up in the Appalachian Mountains.

A lover of hats, she has worn many. Following marriage to her college sweetheart, and as wife, mother, grandmother, teacher, tutor, artist, writer, poet and crafter, she is a lover of art and antiques, surrounding herself, always, with books, seeking to learn more.

In 2015 she authored *Looking for Rainbows, Poetry, Prose and Art*, and in 2017, *Dark Side of the Moon*. Both books of mostly narrative poetry were published by Inner Child Press and were edited by hulya n. yilmaz in 2019, *No Illusions. Through the Looking Glass*, which was nominated to be considered for a Pulitzer Prize by the publisher and editor of Inner Child Press, ltd.

http://www.innerchildpress.com/jackie-davis-allen.php
jackiedavisallen.com

On, and On...

Something there is, that's worthy, priceless,
yet, forbidden. Out of reach; desired nevertheless.

Something that demands an exorbitant cost.
Required, hungered for, of great value. Yet denied.
It's a Something that if pursued, brings one closer
to the brink of certain death.

Something there is, within, demands acknowledgement
A heart filled with wants, needs: a right forbidden.

Something that propels one to strive onward,
toward the light of self improvement.
It's a Something worth risking all that one has
to reach the goal. To claim entitlement's prize.

Something there is, that stands in mind's pathway:
an obstacle, always, rigidly forbidden. Why?

It's Something akin to hunger, thirst, despite,
yes, even to the risk to life. Sadly, boldly,
exacted only from the fairer sex.
Something won? Something lost?

The struggle for attainment continues.
On, and on.

Hope

From the darkness, void of light,
Drip drops of rain. Screams like thunder echo
Between the trills and shrills
of birds, descending now, darker, louder.

Into the leaves of education's stains,
Hope rests uneasily. In the arms of alarm,
there are those singing sorrowful songs
of that which has gone terribly wrong.

From forbidden tenants, rules, dictates,
of pointed mischaracterization, Hope weeps.
Due to lack of empathy, sensitivity, she fades.
Yet, there is one, who swims against tides of desperation.

Disbelieving yet allowing, Hope floats
on education's promise of opportunity:
between strangulation of non-choice and determination.
Midst chaos and its power, Hope is a stranger.

Within hearts of a new generation,
there remains some Hope amongst the remnants.
Is it any wonder that there are now children
who choose to honor Hope's name, Hope's fame?

Yes! There are children everywhere
who sing purposeful songs: the music
of which is Hope's dreams,. And her education's prize.
Despite the past, they claim pieces of Hope as their own.

Make Mine Dark and Strong

Scribbling a line or two, or a stanza,
Make mundane, the horrific, or the beautiful.
Dictate the actuality from life, but from
The muse's rehearsal, say what you will.

From some wisdom or not, I cannot say,
How from pensive minds poems arrive; yet,
If in a moment one gives you pleasure,
A start, or even a thrill, have not the words,

Like ones Webster placed between the pages,
Accomplished their intent, done their duty?

It stands today, that one man's cup of tea
In flavor doesn't have to match any other.
Nor does all verse have to be the same.
And so, if you please, make mine dark and strong.

From Edgar Allan Poe, his writing style,
Strange to some, like a cup of strong tea, black.
Some bitter. Just ask Stephen King what thinks he
Of the lukewarm, feel good, milk toast tomes.

Might he not say, "I'll take mine dark and strong,
And seasoned well with notoriety?"

Tzemin
Ition
Tsai

Dr. Tzemin Ition Tsai comes from the Republic of China(Taiwan). In addition to being a professor of literature at a university, he is more committed to writing poems, novels, and proses. He is also an editor of "Reading, Writing and Teaching" academic text, an International editor of "Contemporary dialogues" literary periodical in Macedonia, and Vice-Chairman of the International Jury of the SAHITTO INTERNATIONAL AWARD in Bangladesh, and a columnist for "Chinese Language Monthly" in Taiwan.

In a wide range of literary creations, he is particularly fond of interesting stories or novels, and writing articles or poems about the feelings of nature and human beings. He has won many national literary awards. His literary works have been anthologized and published in books, journals, and newspapers in more than 55 countries and have been translated into more than 24 languages.

October, That Clock On The Withered Tree

The sun beckoning tears, drop by drop.
Morning light, blooming sighs
On my skin
Mimicking a kind of indistinct elegance
Clock chimes, swaying between near and far.
Visiting in the sea breeze
Searching for the frequent toils of the past few years'
Sing alone all night long,
Dancing in my ears,
Its hands gentle,
A thousand shades of rouge,
Painting my lips.
Shelter, like a weary traveler in the dust,
The vast, boundless sea,
Gaze at the distant, unique wisps of smoke.
Transformed into a warmth.
As close as that seashell,
Silently returning home in the evening.

I Am Left With Only This Paper-Made Soul

Contemplation and obsession
Embrace me
Life murmurs and rushes through
Exploring its own soul
This season
Amidst wild bursts of blue
My heart will
Quiver...!

Coral masquerading as
Insects of lucid dreams
A slow-paced
Underwater ballet
A deep, throbbing
Devotion
The ocean's mighty waves
Swallow their torment

Forget it! Love is also
Swimming away
While moving forward...!"

Lead Your Stone Ox

Tie me to the wind!
Caress my skin!
Heartbeats in symphony, summoning.
A wild night of trysts on the wild shore
Unbridled and untamed
My lightly sketched unwillingness to yield.
At daybreak
Please tell me separately
That was just a
Mirage!

The soul
Sometimes wrinkles.
Like thin paper in someone else's fist
Twisted into a ball.
Like a mystery
Even so, it will revive.
Existing in the gentle packaging of itself
I am left with just this.
Paper-made
Soul!

Shareef Abdur Rasheed

Shareef Abdur Rasheed

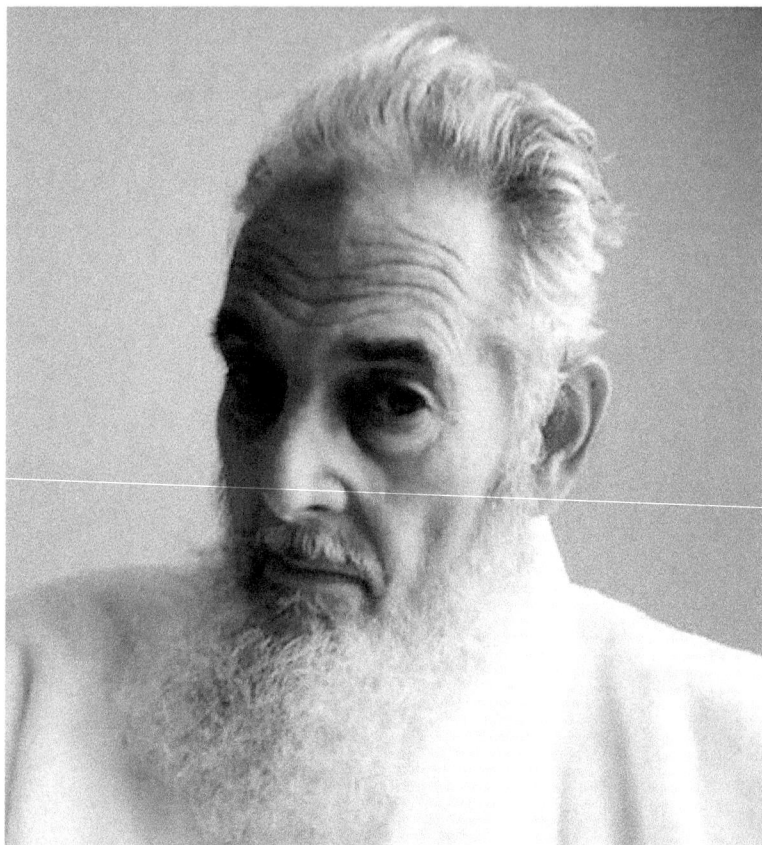

Shareef Abdur-Rasheed, AKA Zakir Flo was born and raised in Brooklyn, New York. His education includes Brooklyn College, Suffolk County Community College and Makkah, Saudi Arabia. He is a Veteran of the Viet Nam era, where in 1969 he reverted to his now reverently embraced Islamic Faith. He is very active in the Islamic community and beyond with his teachings, activism and his humanity.

Shareef's spiritual expression comes through the persona of "Zakir Flo" . Zakir is Arabic for "To remind". Never silent, Shareef Abdur-Rasheed is always dropping science, love, consciousness and signs of the time in rhyme.

Shareef is the Patriarch of the Abdur-Rasheed Family with 9 Children (6 Sons and 3 Daughters) and 41 Grandchildren (24 Boys and 17 Girls).

For more information about Shareef, visit his personal FaceBook Page at :

https://www.facebook.com/shareef.abdurrasheed1
https://zakirflo.wordpress.com

Malala Brave

Born: 1997
Malala Yousafzai
braver than soldiers
stand like mountaintop
advocate education for
girls, women why?
born in Swai, Afghanistan
ruled by Taliban
advocate for females
a suicide move
2012 BAM shot in the head
only 15 years old
went through period of
critical care came through
other side Afghan and Pakistani
national hero
the people's champion
standing redwood strong
airborne rangers pale next to
15 shot in the head by Taliban
come out the other side no fear
come out international, Nobel
Peace Prize winner
youngest in history at 17
now recovered and sought after
world wide
received Canadian citizenship
addressed Canadian house
of Commons
too many accolades to count
well, you get the point
" Don't ever underestimate what
  a child can do "

Peeking under the table

Racism is more American
Then dogshit stink
Just think
Sucker dem love
i mean love like that
Their poster boy for White
Institutional Racism
Don't make no difference
What he do, say
Every word out his ff'ed
Up mouth a lie
Don't hide $hit except for
His $$$$$$$$ yah that's
About it otherwise he hides
In the wide-open spaces
And even tries to overthrow
Whole freaky dicky Govt.
Hidden in broad daylight
Causes 5 capital cops to die
Many of his zombie followers
Go to prison, I mean in the
Thousands
Indicted on more $hit then
Hitler so help me Putin
So, does the Democracy loving???
Poster boy for White
Institutional Supremacy loving
AmeriKKKans dump this narcistic,
Pathological liar?
Their idol who doesn't care
for nothing but him including
his family, kids and all and oooh

Yah including these sick ass
Racist zombies who no matter
What this immoral piece of $#iT
Does still love him because they
as ff'ed as him.
In fact, they are him
AmeriKKKan as apple pie

snakes and rats..,

have side effects. Fact
what you expect from a snake
stand erect, come correct
something else in effect?
remember the Jazz tune
when the snake wiggled his
slick con behind to get in a
women's mind and then she
let him in, felt sorry for him
she forgot what he is and tried
to get what he's not
got bit, said " What? "
like she's surprised
he said " you knew i was a snake "
as she slowly became the " late "
didn't respect the traits
i'll make him something fake
but it's a fact can't change a snake
or a rat
they are just that
including human snakes and rats.
you mean you ain't heard
play with fire, you get burned
check that desire...word

Shareef Abdur Rasheed

Kimberly Burnham

A brain health expert with a PhD in Integrative Medicine, Kimberly Burnham has lived in tropical Colombia; in Belgium during the Vietnam War; in Japan teaching businessmen English; in diverse international Toronto, Canada; and several places in the US. Now, she's in Spokane, WA with her wife, Elizabeth, two sets of twins (age 11 & 14) and three dogs. Her recent book, *Awakenings: Peace Dictionary, Language and the Mind, a Daily Brain Health Program* includes the word for peace in hundreds of languages. Her poetry weaves through 80+ volumes of *The Year of the Poet, Inspired by Gandhi, Women Building the World*, and *A Woman's Place in the Dictionary*. She is currently working on several ekphrastic writing projects. One is a novel, *Art Thief Cracks Healing Code for Parkinson's Disease* and the other is non-fiction, *Using Ekphrastic Fiction Writing and Poetry to Create Interest and Promote Artists, Writers, and Poets*.

http://www.NerveWhisperer.Solutions

https://healthy-brain.medium.com/bears-at-the-window-of-climate-change-d1fb403eeaf3

Malala Fund Remembering the Future

Remember when we were worried about healing
from gun shots and hate
how we survived
then thrived by eliminating conflicts
tackling poverty, discrimination and climate crisis
all the things preventing our girls
from rising within amazing educations

Remember how the girls rose up
supported and cherished
earning places around the world
addressing problems with creative solutions

Remember how we believed in local
educators and activists are the best
how the whole world came
investing in our collective power
driving positive change

Remember when world leaders advocated.
for women and women for themselves
raised into leaders

Remember the world we created together

Education Stolen

In Balochi, a language of Pakistan
"Muhnt" is defined as a share of stolen property
restored to the owner as a peace offering
also defined as the share of the spoils
or rewards for the trouble taken

And I wonder what peace offering
can be returned
when it is education
time learning
that is stolen
how can a few words be returned
when a sense of safety
and accomplishment have been taken
can resilience be returned once stolen

Husbands and Homonyms Across Languages

In Dogri (डोगरी), a language of Pakistan
"रमान" pronounced Raman means peace,
comfort, ease, relaxation, relief, respite, rest
all this in one word
inexplicably the same word means husband
in Maithili, another language of Pakistan
would that all husbands and wives could create
a feeling of peace for themselves and their families
imagine a good man
taking his daughters to school
where they learn of the world
theirs and the rest
in peace and ease
returning home safely to do terrific deeds
in their community and beyond

Elizabeth E. Castillo

Elizabeth Esguerra Castillo is a multi-awarded and an Internationally-Published Contemporary Author/Poet and a Professional Writer / Creative Writer / Feature Writer / Journalist / Travel Writer from the Philippines. She has 2 published books, "Seasons of Emotions" (UK) and "Inner Reflections of the Muse", (USA). Elizabeth is also a co-author to more than 60 international anthologies in the USA, Canada, UK, Romania, India. She is a Contributing Editor of Inner Child Magazine, USA and an Advisory Board Member of Reflection Magazine, an international literary magazine. She is a member of the American Authors Association (AAA) and PEN International.

Web links:

Facebook Fan Page

https://free.facebook.com/ElizabethEsguerraCastillo

Google Plus

https://plus.google.com/u/0/+ElizabethCastillo

One Girl Who Changed the World

Malala, a name that would go down in history-
Coined as an International Symbol of the Fight for Girl's
Education
Being shot was not a hindrance for her, not a restriction
Young as she was,
She continued her noble advocacy.

The youngest ever to win the Noble Peace Prize,
For her to be known across the globe is not a surprise
"One child, one teacher, one book, and one pen can change
the world"
Malala proved that being young is not an excuse to do great
things for others.

Courage to be True

Do you have to hide your true self?
Make pretensions, be under disguise?
To be noticed by others, do you have to lie?
Look yourself in the mirror and ask yourself why?
Has the world made a slave out of you
That once you feel unappreciated,
You succumb to being blue?
In reality, those who don a mask,
Are the ones who don't know authentic happiness
For out of the mundane things, their joy dwells.
Living each day in their own make-believe world,
Lost souls, restless hearts, crying for freedom
To break free from the chains that bind
And to have the courage to be true to mankind.
Clowns are sent to entertain the crowd,
But beneath the thick layers of hues
Can we say that their smiles are true?
The funny comedian in the movies that we see
In real life emerges a depressed soul once alone
For behind the laughter, behind the cheer,
We can't see their real selves, can't see the hidden fear.
True, happy people don't have to mask their true selves,
For they don't seek validation or appreciation from others,
Simply by being their own self, being honest about what
they feel,
Open doors of love and acceptance for those who truly
care.

Indigo Child

i am not of this world -
i came from an abysmal chaos-
but from this beautiful chaos, Desiderata was born-
a child of the Universe, precious and golden
a lovely old soul beyond time and space-
often misunderstood by mediocre minds-
but applauded by great free thinkers -
i long for a world enveloped in serenity-
inhabited by empaths with great sensitivity
a loner I may be but this is who I am-
but i've got this deep connection with things around me
an indigo girl at birth-
my temporary sanctuary is the Earth
lone wolves gather at my feet-
for i am their Goddess in human form.

Joe
Paire

Joe Paire

Joseph L Paire' aka Joe DaVerbal Minddancer . . .
is a quiet man, born in a time where civil liberties
were a walk on thin ice. He's been a victim of his
own shyness often sidelined in his own quest for
love. He became the observer, charting life's path.
Taking note of the why, people do what they do. His
writings oft times strike a cord with the
dormant strings of the reader. His pen the rosined
bow drawn across the mind. He comes full-frontal
or in the subtlest way, always expressing in a way
that stimulate the senses.

www.facebook.com/joe.minddancer

At The Age Of 17

Many people from my era,
didn't care to get involved.
Too much faith in the government,
To get things solved.

We had our activist, activity.
We've had our acts against our civil liberties
We have our facts, how life should be.
How could we ignore what grants us peace.

Human rights in times of human strife
At times, and most times.
At the cost of human lives.
Malala Yousafzai realized at the age of 17
She became the youngest to receive,
A Nobel prize.

The Taliban at times,
banned girls from attending schools
(we're in need of some advocacy,
To keep our own history as a rule)

But I digress, not to dismiss but address,
The unrest. This is not a test,
Or an isolated incident. Her story is our story

Can we survive, and rise to a level of,
Peace without incident?

Can I Reach You?

Can I relay my experience,
the same way you'll experience it
the way my parents delivered it..

I was nay all the way,
until those very words became evident
emotionally relevant,
old folks can't tell you.
wish you would've listened
but that's the part I'm missing

I want to get past the "yeah right"
And "I hear ya Unc"
I want to appeal to your zeal
And avoid malevolent zealots
How do we teach the similarities
Without discussing polarities.

Parallel lives, or history repeats itself
It's time to realize
History doesn't read itself
And philosophy well,
future minds often find
the truth within themselves

I'm just trying to help the process
When I've been through your synopsis
Forget the optics, not the topic
Times have changed, not to the point of tossing
Can we gather together, to do a little talking

Job Application

I was on a vacation, blessed with relations
Life had its own idea of fun
Friendless in an endless amount of strife
Soon to take a wife I no better deserved,
Then, I confessed then.

Rest in peace means I sleep well
I'm in a deep well
I need a job, that means a background check
That means a credit reference
Lord knows I got no sense or no cents
Since as long as a simile would fit, this riff

Fitness, can you lift fifty pounds
Can you work weekends at any hour
And come in if you're out of town
(I'm just trying to fry up some ground round)

Have you ever been convicted, or currently indited
I got excited,
I was delighted they asked that question
(I mean it's not like I'm running for president
I'm thinking fry cook when I'm not booked
I'm thinking equal justice under the flaw
I spelt the law wrong on purpose
But a porpoise isn't a fish.

It's a whale of a tale I'll tell you
Oh, I got the job with a certified stamp
And that job is rubbish.

hülya
n.
yılmaz

hülya n. yılmaz

Professor Emerita, hülya n. yılmaz is a published author, literary translator, and Co-Chair and Director of Editing Services at Inner Child Press International. Her poetic work appeared in numerous anthologies of global endeavors and was presented at various literary events in the U.S. and abroad. In 2018, WIN honored yılmaz with an award of excellence. Since 2017, her two poems remain permanently installed in *Telepoem Booth* – a U.S.-wide poetic art exhibition. hülya finds it vital for everyone to seek a deeper sense of self, and writes creatively to attain a comprehensive awareness for and development of our humanity.

hülya n. yılmaz, a traveler on the journey called "life" . . .

Writing Web Site
https://hulyanyilmaz.com/

Editing Web Site
https://hulyasfreelancing.com

Point Blank

Shot in the head in her school bus
at the age of 15 . . .

Malala Yousuafzai survived the barbaric attack
not only to live on,
but to become and be a role model
for women across the globe;
women who were brutalized
in one way or another.

Much has been written about her.
She wrote much about her experience.
Talked, she has aplenty.
Human rights, educational rights,
civil rights, and women's rights
are the focal points of her activism today.

One wonders . . .
what would she, could she do
when American women are concerned.

If only there were a Malala Yousafzai
under the female umbrellas of the U.S.

"Honor" Killings

What is there left to do,
when a grandfather, a father, an uncle
or a brother (younger or older)
sees it justified to kill a female family member
in the name of "honor"? An older woman
often condones that murder, after all! A grandmother,
a mother or an aunt who has been equally brainwashed
as the men of the same household, holding
double standards for "honor" when it comes
to the womenfolk . . .

Where does it say that men can and do live
without "honor"?

Better yet . . .
how can anyone define "honor" succicntly?

"Honor" killings . . . only women allowed!

When Love Kills

A newspaper article
reported the carnage:

A pregnant woman
was stoned to death in public.
Proudly, her brothers
admitted to the murder.
They had sentenced her to death,
because she became a stain
on the family's honor.
She married a man
of her own choice.

How dare she fell in love with a man
outside her clan's approval?

Teresa E. Gallion

Teresa E. Gallion was born in Shreveport, Louisiana and moved to Illinois at the age of 15. She completed her undergraduate training at the University of Illinois Chicago and received her master's degree in Psychology from Bowling Green State University in Ohio. She retired from New Mexico state government in 2012.

She moved to New Mexico in 1987. While writing sporadically for many years, in 1998 she started reading her work in the local Albuquerque poetry community. She has been a featured reader at local coffee houses, bookstores, art galleries, museums, libraries, Outpost Performance Space, the Route 66 Festival in 2001 and the State of Oklahoma's Poetry Festival in Cheyenne, Oklahoma in 2004. She occasionally hosts an open mic.

Teresa's work is published in numerous Journals and anthologies. She has two CDs: *On the Wings of the Wind* and *Poems from Chasing Light.* She has published three books: *Walking Sacred Ground, Contemplation in the High Desert* and *Chasing Light.*

Chasing Light was a finalist in the 2013 New Mexico/Arizona Book Awards.

The surreal high desert landscape and her personal spiritual journey influence the writing of this Albuquerque poet. When she is not writing, she is committed to hiking the enchanted landscapes of New Mexico. You may preview her work at

http://bit.ly/1aIVPNq or *http://bit.ly/13IMLGh*

Malala Humanitarian

Some youths are born to defy adults
that do not address critical needs of girls.
Malala's courage to help women pursue
education led to a bullet to her face.

That did not deter her commitment to open
the doors of education denied to females.
She remains an activist for women
with determination beyond her years.

The youngest Nobel Prize humanitarian,
she captured the world's attention
and holds strong the passion
to address the rights of the female gender.

Soar Like an Eagle

The waves dance for me today.
What a flamboyant flirt.
But I cannot follow them out to sea.
It is not my time to walk on water.

The Spirits encircle me.
Tell me to step back, enjoy the view.
Let the sand massage the feet.

Time sits on the horizon.
Will be there for you
in the appropriate season.

Go forth, enjoy nature's offerings.
Your respect for dear Mother
has earned you the rite of passage
into her beautiful places.

You may soar like an eagle
across Mother's land.
Grab the love streams
caressing you in sacred wind.

Words to Love You

I want these words to love you.
I Scroll them across the page.
An offering to the universe
for all ears able to receive.

Because

I want these words to love you.
Lift you up in times of distress.
Push you forward when you want
to run away from the challenge.

Because

I want these words to love you
when you freeze at the gates of fear.
And push you through with
the heat of love in each syllable.

Because

I want these words to love you.
Squeeze the impurity from your veins
to help you walk lightly
on your journey against the wind.

Because

I want these words to love you.
Keep you eternally warm.
Rub your legs with stamina
to carry you through the storm.

Because

I want these words to love you
and bring you to me.
I am dancing on the horizon
waiting to capture your smile.

Because

I love you.

Teresa E. Gallion

Ashok K. Bhargava

ASHOK BHARGAVA is a poet, writer, inspirational speaker and a literary consultant. He has attended poetry conferences in Italy, Turkey, India and Philippines. His latest book "Riding the Tide" about his battle with cancer has been translated and published in Arabic, Hindi, Telugu and Bengali languages. He is a contributing writer to several anthologies worldwide including World Poetry Almanac 2014. He has been published in numerous print and online magazines.

Ashok has won many accolades including Poet Ambassador to Japan, Kalidasa International award, World Poetry Lifetime Achievement award, Writers Beyond Borders Peace award and Tapsilog Leadership award for his community involvement. He is founder of Writers International Network Canada Society to discover, nourish, recognize and celebrate writers, poets and artists and to assist them to network with the community at large. He is the author of eight books of poetry and one anthology. He is Artist-in-Residence at Moberly Arts & Cultural Centre and also co-edits the literary section of The Link Newspaper.

Why

carefree
giggles
in the back
seat of school bus
ended abruptly
when someone
someone shouted
who is Malala.

A man with Kalashnikovs
red eyes and hand-rolled
turban
a silhouette of darkness
ignorance
Taliban, al-Qaeda.

Her gleeful response
"I am Malala"
met bang-bang-bang

horrified
muffled cries
blood soaked kids
hid under the seats.

He left
with a victorious smile.

Questioning
why did this happen
could be an opening
into understanding
why.

We Can If We Want

With my little eyes
I see God everywhere.
In the misery of the poor and
The abundance of the rich.
I see him in the eyes of refugees
Pouring in like sand grains
In an hourglass and slip through the borders.

I feel him in the cries of raped women
Out loud before every sunrise.

I see him amongst
The Latino caravans and Haitian leaky boats
Trying to enter the USA.

I see him in the war zones of Syria, Iraq,
Afghanistan and Ukraine.
Let's not burn them to ashes
in the name of God.
We can light peace
if we really want to.
We can heal the desperate
if we want to

Look Inside

There is
as much
in
that little
space within
the heart
as there is
in the whole
world
outside.

Heaven, earth, fire, wind
Sun, moon, stars
whatever
is
and
whatever
is not
everything is
there
inside.

Caroline 'Ceri Naz' Nazareno Gabis

Caroline 'Ceri' Nazareno-Gabis

Caroline 'Ceri Naz' Nazareno-Gabis, author of Velvet Passions of Calibrated Quarks, World Poetry Canada International Director to Philippines is a multi-awarded poet, editor, journalist, educator, peace and women's advocate. She believes that learning other's language and culture is a doorway to wisdom.

Among her poetic belts include **Gabrielle Galloni Memorial Panorama International Youth Award 2022,** Panorama Youth Literary Awards 2020, 7th Prize Winner in the 19th, 20th and 21st Italian Award of Literary Festival; Writers International Network-Canada ''Amazing Poet 2015'', The Frang Bardhi Literary Prize 2014 (Albania), Poet Journalist Award 2014 (Tuzla, Istanbul, Turkey) and World Poetry Empowered Poet 2013 (Vancouver, Canada). She's a featured member of Association of Women's Rights and Development (AWID), The Poetry Posse, Galaktika Poetike, Asia Pacific Writers and Translators (APWT), Axlepino and Anacbanua. Her poetry and children's stories have been featured in different anthologies and magazines worldwide.

Links to her works:

http://panitikan.ph/2018/03/30/caroline-nazareno-gabis/

https://apwriters.org/author/ceri_naz/

http://www.aveviajera.org/nacionesunidasdelasletras/id1181.html

Malalai of Maiwand

Malala, you are a true heroine
Proclaimed as Youngest Nobel Prize Laureate
Blossomed from his father's thoughts
 and humanitarian works,
You were loved, Malala.
You woke up those wounded spirits
Who were buried in deep slumber
Of fear, hopelessness and vanished dreams,
Your advocacy on education for girls
And human rights have transformed
The leaders and the youth,
Your light shine in all corners of the globe.

hidden treasure

you left to win and gain
lasting memories,
exhilarating captures
when nature calls,
from sweeping meanders,
from the lush of greens,
from the sulfury smell
of the enthralling coast,
 from the intimate sacred chamber,
that replenishes & sanctifies
wounded souls,
from all walks of life,
been here and there,
sometimes lost,
but never forsaken;
for always
you are the treasure
from the forest of words.

Decoding the Academic Regalia and "Abaray na Dayew"

Behind the cameras, tears poured down,
but it meant a glorious victory over grief, stress,
 anxieties and obstacles.
Behind those filtered smiles,
 I missed my lost loved ones.
I am offering this achievement to them.
The value of encouragement, empowerment,
 and dedication were my powerhouse
 to move forward to finish this journey;
 there was a lag, but I believed, there is always time.
I fervently prayed for guidance,
patience, courage, and determination
 for I trusted the process
because a monumental change
is just right behind the rainbows of willpower;
The John Knox's cap over our heads,
the gowns embracing our bodies,
 with the emblems inspired by the rule of time,
honor, our heritage, and privileges
 remind us how great the change has been,
until we walk the road for a while,
looking back, we see how far we have come
the odyssey to humility and the heart of humanity.

Swapna Behera

Swapna Behera is a trilingual poet, translator, environmentalist, editor from India and author of seven books of different genres including one on children's literature on Environment. She is the recipient of International UGADI AWARD 2019, honoured from Gujurat Sahitya Akademi 2022, 2021 International Poesis Award of Honor as Jury, Pentasi B World Fellow Poet, Honoured Poet of India from Seychelles Government and International awards from Algeria, Morocco, Kajhakhstan, modern Arabic Literary Renaissance of Egypt, International Arts Council Argentina etc. Her stories, poems, articles are published in many International and National magazines and ezines. Her poem A NIGHT IN THE REFUGEE CAMP is translated into 67 languages. She has received over 60 National and International Awards. At present she is the Cultural Ambassador for India and South Asia of Inner Child and the life member of Odisha Environmental Society

Email
swapna.behera@gmail.com

Web Site
http://swapnabehera.in/

81

I am Malala : the Phoenix

the sizzling voice from the epicentre whispers---
give me a book , a teacher ,a pen
I can give you the eternal smile
a smile that gives a choice,
choice to live and love,
fly or swim,
earn fame and never a shame
put on the dawn, and never a dusk
 choice to be pregnant or to be my own self,
lend my skill or express my agony
choice to be secured,
rejuvenate my ambition and desires
choice to be a virgin or a mother,
my existence is the burning lava in the time zone
I am not a slave of the terrorists
fanaticism and vandalism down down !
you may shoot a bullet to my forehead
I am a wonder woman and a thunder woman
my blood will write document of peace and education
the epitaph of kindness
I am MALALA
by the way ; I know
how to deal violence with my voice

Jayanta Mohapatra : when his silence echoes

can a legacy ever die?
the audacity of your verses echo
 in the rustling leaves of the bamboo tree
that stands in "CHANDRABHAGA"
a poet and his soliloquy entwine there
though not too rebel
you observed the deaths in Orissa ,
sagging floor of summer nights
sermons of the garbage heap
you can never die
 your poems can never say where you are
you are local in sync with the globe
your silence is transmitted to poetry
introvert and solitary ,highly impulsive
as your empathy is your poetry
a perineal river, a flash in the horizon
a contented soul so gracious
giving justice to common man and seminars
a physics professor yet your poetry
with all conviction justifies solitude ,metaphors
mystery are narratives
and time plays the theme of relationship
poetry is like an ongoing give and take actions
woman as you define
" even when she is
even when she is not "
you reflect socialism
 observe hunger from the twisted throat
 ready to suffer as penance
staring at your own door overpowered by time

you are secular, a meditator . transmitter of the jungles ,life
the graveyard, crowds ,love, whorehouse in a Calcutta
street
hunger ,missing persons all move around your axis
so do the myth and mystery
the solitude is your honest confessions
the left side of life dazzles as innocently as your right voice
you exist here and there in each heart
at the time line of all holocausts
 your silence echoes

*Dedicated to Jayanta Mohapatra (22 October 1928- 27
August 2023) the Indian poet born in Cuttack ,Odisha.He
is the first Indian poet to win a Sahitya Akademi Award for
English ,He was awarded a Padmashri the fourth highest
civilian honour in India but he returned it.*

bouncing shadow.....

the deciduous shadow
bouncing on the ominous riverine
as chronicles of
undefined sin
oozing blood
sprinkles the anecdotes of life
with lofty promises
the mayhem of Being
stabs it's own self
to dive into the profound senses
a chime of laconic leaves
the obscure reflection
of mundane existence
dies millions of times
to proclaim everlasting spring - -

Albert
'Infinite'
Carrasco

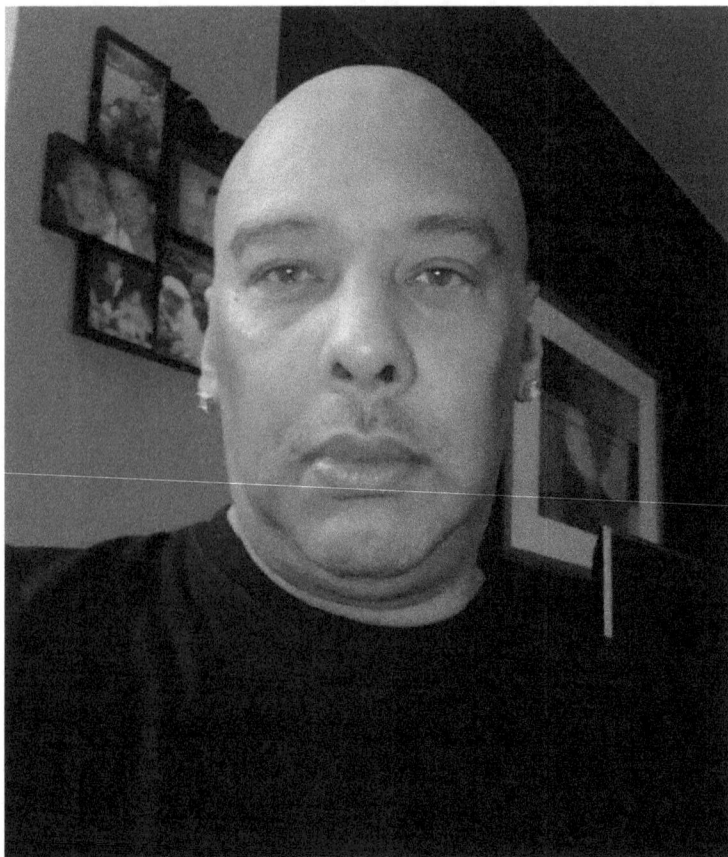

Albert "Infinite The Poet" Carrasco is an urban poet, mentor and public speaker.

Albert believes his experience of growing up in poverty, dealing with drugs and witnessing murder over and over were lessons learnt, in order to gain knowledge to teach. Albert's harsh reality and honesty is a powerfully packed punch delivered through rhyme. Infinite grew up in the east part of the Bronx and still resides there, so he knows many young men will follow the same dark path he followed looking for change. The life of crime should never be an option to being poor but it is, very often.

Infinite poetry @lulu.com

Alcarrasco2 on YouTube

Infinite the poet on reverbnation

Infinite Poetry

http://www.lulu.com/us/en/shop/al-infinite-carrasco/infinite-poetry/paperback/product-21040240.html

Malala Yousafzi

Men and women alike should have equal rights, since the Taliban took control of my town in Pakistan. i took a stand to speak out and shed light. We couldn't watch television or listen to our favorite music station, that was awful. If we did and was caught, the punishment would be harsh because disobedience was unlawful. Education for girls was also banned but luckily for me, my father was a teacher. IN 2008 I left my classmates not knowing when I would see them again, if ever. Education was something i yearned, in 2012 i started to speak out about publicly on behalf of the right for girls to learn. that would become my passion.

In October 2012 I was on my way home from school when a masked gunman entered my school bus and asked, who is Malala? when he found out it was me, he shot me in the head leaving me for dead. I woke up ten days later in a hospital in Birmingham, England. The doctors explained to me about the tragedy and that the world was praying for a speedy recovery. After months of surgeries and rehabilitation I met with my family in our new home in the United Kingdom. It was then when I knew I had a choice, either lay low or continue my fight for education using my voice.

I did great! i established the Malala fund, a charity to give every girl opportunity and in 2014 I became the youngest ever Nobel Laureate. In 2018 I began studying Politics, Economics and Philosophy, IN 2020 I graduated from Oxford University.

Do better

We have to do better. Reach out to people you grew up with because life is short, people are fighting demons of all sorts, depression, addiction, loneliness, unhealthy thoughts, etcetera etcetera. We can't assume people are doing okay because during the time of assumption people are slipping away. Some individuals reach out, others stray. Some pop up, text or call, others feel like they're stuck between four closing walls. Mask are being worn. Silent suffering is common, I can't let the world see my pain... I can't let my problems become someone else's problem... no one cares... people are happy that i'm in this position... are thoughts while they battle their demon. Look at him, he's doing good. Look at her, she's doing well. Look at all of them, they're all fine. When is it going to be my time? Everything you see isn't always what it is, nowadays almost everything is sensationalized, especially social media with its visual lies. Made up lifestyles go viral while others feel like they're not keeping up with the status quo so the earths rotation sends them into a downward spiral.

Don't go

Many men didn't want me to retire and raise my kids, that didn't suit em, that wasn't detrimental to their income, they wanted me to keep raising my children sauer along with smith and wesson for protection, it was beneficial to them if I stood in the hood buss'n mine and Chopin cookies to nickels and dimes. Ayo Inf I need about a six month run, I need you to hold me down in these trapped up slums, take a block by swingn that shit like a sword, let me and my team live and we'll pay you rent like a landlord, ayo inf can I get a shift, they needed money drip and godfather spliffs. I let em all eat, I wasn't turning my back on anyone, if I win we all won, plus I knew how hard it was to come up in these BX streets. I put that time in, put that work in, in the hood and the kitchen, I went through it all, got caked up, hit up, locked up, fell and came back up, plus, I buried most of the men with whom I came up. There was nothing left to witness but my own death, so I left before soul theft.

Michelle

Joan

Barulich

Michelle Joan Barulich

94

Michelle Joan Barulich was born in Honolulu, Hawaii on the island of Oahu. She started writing poetry and songs with her younger brother Paul. They have written many songs in their teen years. She is currently studying Alternative Medicine and would like to become a Homeopathic Doctor. Michelle loves all kinds of animals and birds; she does wild rehabilitation. She has also rescued rock pigeons that make great pets.

https://www.facebook.com/michelle.barulich

Malala

You are an inspiration

A global icon of courage

A teacher and a leader

To help guide, and teach

Your bravery is astounding.

Your journey is remarkable

To empower women

And to fight the resistance

For the education of women.

The Silent Wind

Where I used to know where I wanted to go
And where I used to know where I wanted to roam
The news came on a sunny day
And that's where it all seems to end
Now, tell me where do I begin?
What do I do with my life now?
What do I do? and where do I go?
Can't seem to picture your love has gone away
I can feel the pain in my heart and mind
Can't seem to shake it off.
I wear the mask you have sewn together for me
And where I used to know where I wanted to roam
Run, run with the silent wind behind me
Can't escape to another world
Can't seem to find death when I seek it
The hours seem so long
I walk into the distant halls
Where the candles burn for you, for me
The softness of the music
Takes me to you in another time world
..And where I used to know;
Where I wanted to go
And where I used to know where I wanted to roam..

Horse's Spirit

I see them runnin' into the night
Try to catch one if you can
They have fire in their eyes
They have fire in their soul
And the waves are falling down
As they run behind the purple skies
I envy them, they are the masters of their own defeat
They cross their destiny
Though they have no boundaries
You can't track them down
They are just too fast
Runnin' wild and free
To see them astonishes me
Beauty and style they have it all
Oh, horse's spirit
Will you ever let me love you?,,,,

Eliza Segiet

Eliza Segiet graduated with a Master's Degree in Philosophy at Jagiellonian University.
Received *Global Literature Guardian Award* – from Motivational Strips, World Nations

Writers' Union and Union Hispanomundial De Escritores (UHE) 2018.

Nominated for the Pushcart Prize 2019, 2021.

Laureate *Naji Naaman Literary Prize 2020, International Award Paragon of Hope* (2020),

World Award 2020 *Cesar Vallejo* for Literary Excellence.

Laureate of the Special Jury *Sahitto International Award* 2021, World Award *Premiul Fănuş Neagu* 2021.

Finalist *Golden Aster Book* World Literary Prize 2020, *Mili Dueli* 2022, Voci nel deserto 2022.

At the international Festival of Poetry CAMPIONATO MONDIALE DI POESIA (2021/2022) she won the title of vice-champion of the world.

Award BHARAT RATNA RABINDRANATH TAGORE INTERNATIONAL AWARD (2022).

Creating oneself
To Malala Yousafzai

Education should be
Everyone's food
– for it is what leads
to the horizons of existence.

When what was previously forbidden
becomes the power force to fight,

it is when a new beginning starts.

To begin,
without looking at the odds

– to say enough to illiteracy!
– to make those who push gender equality out of their
minds
realise that:

Adam and Eve
have the same rights!

The rights which
transformed and imbued with knowledge
will be able to create themselves anew,
to find a previously inaccessible tract.
To be able to choose
between knowledge and ignorance
– is to awake a sleeping mind.

To be in touch with the world of words and signs
is to experience the fullness of one's time.

Then the bumpy road will be left behind,
the paths paved with the fragrance of wisdom will allow
you to

– Be and Live, with an abundance of sensations.

Translated by Dorota Stępińska

The Path to Knowledge

Cactus-like, prickly impotence
provokes one to search,
to ask questions.
An incomplete answer will be:
a 'perhaps',
whose complement
will bear more dilemmas
bringing about a new quality.
Those who cannot find answers
keep on searching.

Will they find them?

There may be some
who
will never accept the
state of unawareness
of all the lights and shadows of our existence,
the hollowed-out darkness of their own bewilderment.

Perhaps the Socratic
— *I know that I know nothing*
is not an agony of the mind,
but a guiding star
for taking further steps
illuminating the path to knowledge.

Translated by Dorota Stępińska

Mr M.
In the memory of Czesław Miłosz

Enriched by experiences
of not only her own life,
she became cautious.
Observing others
how zestfully they bask in
other people's victories.

The same ones
who before pretended
they did not know who Mr M. was,
now, when he'd been awarded
with the most renown prize
they suddenly remembered him,
even the friendships they'd shared.

Censored in his own land,
'buried' when alive,
'resurrected' after the Nobel Prize.

Translated by Dorota Stępińska

William S. Peters Sr.

Bill's writing career spans a period of over 50 years. Being first Published in 1972, Bill has since went on to Author in excess of 50 additional Volumes of Poetry, Short Stories, etc., expressing his thoughts on matters of the Heart, Spirit, Consciousness and Humanity. His primary focus is that of Love, Peace and Understanding!

Bill says . . .

I have always likened Life to that of a Garden. So, for me, Life is simply about the Seeds we Sow and Nourish. All things we "Think and Do", will "Be" Cause and eventually manifest itself to being an "Effect" within our own personal "Existences" and "Experiences" . . . whether it be Fruit, Flowers, Weeds or Barren Landscapes! Bill highly regards the Fruits of his Labor and wishes that everyone would thus go on to plant "Lovely" Seeds on "Good Ground" in their own Gardens of Life!

to connect with Bill, he is all things Inner Child

www.iaminnerchild.com

Personal Web Site

www.iamjustbill.com

Malala

They asked . . .
Why would a woman pursue an education.
Of what use would it be
Simply to be a Housewife, Mother of Lover.

Be mindful they said,
But you did not listen,
For your mind
Was that of your own,
And you wanted to expand
Beyond
What pothers had dictated
Your life to be about . . .

BOOM, you disturbed our peace,
So,
BOOM, we shot you
To make a point,
But that did not deter you

You took one for the team
Of righteousness,
And we can no longer hold the reins,
For you are celebrated,
Educated
Beyond our feeble comprehension

Congratulations
On your Nobel Prize

A Poem in the Making

I want to be lyrical.
I want to be well versed
In the use of a language
That is uplifting,
Informative,
Experiential

I at times wish to rhyme,
Other times not

Some times there is a magic
Hidden in the subterfuge
Of chaos and discordance

I want to transport my readers,
My observers
Into a place, a space
Within themselves
Where a common resonance
Is found between us

I want to heighten our sensitivities
To the fact
That though we are the building blocks
Of this world, this existence,
It and the world remains
Bigger than us

I want to espouse such things,
Such thoughts,
Such emotions
That inspires each of us,
Myself included
To expand, to expand, to expand

I want to invoke thoughtfulness and smiles,
Unmitigated laughter and love,
Contemplation, consideration and compassion

I want to weave and offer
A cloak of humility
That we all can wear

I am searching
For a humanity
That does not falter
When the Sun goes down,
Or when shadows and darkness
Creeps stealthily into our
Sphere of influence

I want to get to intimately know you,
And you, I... the lesser,
And the potential
Of what we collectively
Can become

These things are possible, truly,
For I have read the verse and lyrics
Of others, and
I am truly beyond measure
AMAZED
.....
and i sincerely believe
That not only I,
But we all
Are simply
A Poem in the making.

Isn't that just magnificently grand?

A House on Fire

This is my home.
It was the home of my ancestors,
And yours as well.

What will our children,
And our children's children
Ad infinitum
Inherit

Greed the avarice
And covetous postures
Have put it all
In danger of a ominous change
Or destruction,
And our silence condoned
This coming end ...
.....
But it does not have to be that way,
Does it?

Yes there are still
Beautiful sunsets and sunrises,
Flowers and trees and birds
And butterflies.

We also have the mountains,
The skies
And the valleys
And our tremendously at risk
Streams and rivers, seas and oceans,
Not to mention

The air we MUST breathe
That we may live ...
But live how?

The House is on Fire

October

2023

Featured Poets

~ * ~

CSP Shrivastava

Huniie Parker

Noreen Snyder

Ramkrishna Paul

i FLY

because I Can

. . . said the Dreamer to the world.

www.iamjustbill.com

CSP

Shrivastava

Mr. CSP Shrivastava, a seasoned bilingual poet has authored a book 'Shekhar's Poetic Musings'. His poems have been published nationally and internationally. He has received several awards including Gujrat Sahitya Academy Award - 2021 @2022 besides the award of Rabindra Nath Tagore Literary Honors from the Seychelles Government.

Wherefrom fragrances of flowers come ?

Wherefrom fragrances of flowers come
And wherefrom brilliance of Sun ?

The fluidity of river
The constituents of air ?

The presence of stony mass
Or, in entirety the essence of cosmos ?

For these never be in the run
It's from within, within as a sum

The sum of your being
Collecting nectar of love and growing

It's your love from inner core so profound
Which in peace eternally echoes & resounds.

The bliss is all yours

What I perceive n see through naked eyes
A perfect ambience none denies

While soaring thro' high skies
Like when a bird merrily flies

Or, Whoso or whereat they peep thro' n magnify
It's the same game, the same lap that can mollify

A soul weary of myriads of miseries
Missing the magnificence n treasuries

Frequenting the forbidden follies n falsities
In exuberance of possible possibilities

At the end, the long last...
Breathes the bliss to ever last

When the soul in acceptance lies
All in belief to the fathomless closing all eyes.

It's umpteen times that so you do.

The ripened age of grace
Brilliance and sparkling face
A brief to the unclear posterity
Accumulated stock of austerity

Something whispered to soul
A premonition of pranced whole
The restless soul with turbulence
Promised excellence of exuberance

A relentless conspiracy to eternally tempt
Midst mortifying frequent repeat of dent
It's the unique yearnings of the race
To harken back to primordial trace

Men consistently crave to crawl
For the myriads of worldly foul
Blind to the real inner plea
With a wrongful glee

It's umpteen times
That so you do...

Huniie

Parker

Huniie Parker

Huniie Holly aka Huniie'z Xpressionz is a poet, Spoken Word artist and so much more. She is a spiritual based writer who is very active in the poetry community. She has an open door policy when it comes to assisting others.

She can be found on FaceBook at :
www.facebook.com/Huniie

Stop by and give here a read.

The Blind Can't Lead the Blind

Hey, been saying I'm Nzpired but how can I be?
When I haven't seen my own vision for the trees?
If I can't see for me
How can I have hopes of seeing for you?
Always heard the blind can't lead the blind
Didn't understand that meant me
Thought because of my heart
I was able to see
First the homeless man,
then the mother taking the two by four upside the head
just to protect her babies
The drug addict in so much mental and emotional pain
Trying to become numb
I knew they all needed rescuing
But so, did I
Blind people can't lead blind people
See there is only one that can rescue
Though he needs vessels
Soldiers that are wounded on the battlefield are sent home
for a reason
It takes some Army, Airforce and Marines
Even wisdom to know when to fall back
It's ok to breath
So, no longer I, we, walk with tunnel vision
Binoculars are a tool, but even they
Can't look ahead and see side to side at the same time
Soldiers on different levels
All dealing with our own devils
Glasses are sometimes necessary
Because the blind can't lead the blind.

Small Beginnings Make Great Endings

Funny how someone recently
Told me God said NOT to despise small beginnings
How those small beginnings
Are going to bring Great Endings

What are your small beginnings?
Jesus had a small beginning
In a manger, in a barn
He was a King

Queens rise up
Small beginnings is where your foundation
Is Laid
To prepare you for Great Endings

Esther took a year to sit
Preparing for
Her debut of
Great Endings

Though Queen of Queens
Maybe born
It's through the fire
You come out as pure gold

When milk is churned is
When cream rises to the top
So, hold your head up
You are the cream of the crop

Queen of Queens
Adorned in your anointing

Draped in the finest clay
The potter's hand could find

To shape and mold
Into a totally unique
Being
Queen of Queens

Walk I the path only your
Footsteps can fit
While others wonder in amazement
HOW?

But do not despise
 SMALL BEGINNINGS
THAT MAKE
GREAT ENDINGS!

Isadshi-Koseshi Female Warrior Arises

I dragged my feet through the ashes.
as I looked around me
head hung low.
scalp shaved.
all my glory was gone,
as they snatched me
tied my hands and feet,
and throwed me in the cage,
time after time I escaped,
fought war after war,
molestation,
rape,
depression,
attacked my body mind and soul,
destroy her is the cry that arose around me,
all the while sitting in my corner,
head bowed,
I called his name silently to myself,
finding a strength, they knew nothing of,
I Isadshi-Koseshi,
Female Warrior,
hid withing,
screaming,
gathered my strength,
studied my enemies,
gathered my weapons,
allowed them to think,
I was defeated,
let them pet my head,
appeared harmless,
as I gained in strength,

while they took me through test after test,
stripping me of all they thought they could,
not understanding,
like the Phoenix,
I to will arise out of my ashes,
as I step forth,
strength arises,
fills me,
from the depth of my soul,
he has poured out his anointing,
has called me forth,
with my sword,
I arise,
I stand,
I am,
Isadshi-Koseshi female warrior,
Until it is my time,
your attacks,
only make me stronger,
for I cannot be taken down,
until HE says so!

Noreen

Snyder

Noreen Snyder

Noreen Ann Snyder is a poet and a published author of five poetry books with four of them are co-authored with her loving husband, Garry A. Snyder. She will always do what she can to honor her loving husband, Garry Snyder, and keep him alive. In his honor she founded The Poetry Club and Facebook Live every Saturday evening. She is the host of "Have a Chat With Poet Noreen", monthly show. Noreen loves to read and to write poetry.

Accept Me — I'm Childless

Do you have any children?—
I hate this question!
It's inevitable...
people you meet, surveys,
doctors, and hospitals.
This question won't go away.
When you're childless,
it's a pain, heartbreaking to answer
and you got to keep your head up
and your feelings locked inside.
You want to explode and say,
"It's none of your business"
but instead quietly you say no.
No one knows the hurt, the anger,
the pain, the heartbreak you go through
except for the ones who are childless.
Each childless person deals
with it differently.
Then you have to deal with
some cold-hearted ones
who degraded you so low
they say there's something wrong with you
because all womwn had children.
That is bull!
I'm not the only one!
Stop degrading me and the others!

Accept Me — I'm Childless

I am not childless by choice
and do not ask me why—
it's none of your business.
It took me years to accept it

still I have my bad days.
I am ME!
Accept me for who I am or
go away and leave me alone!
I know God loves me
just the way I am.
I know my man loves me
just the way I am.
God knows what He was doing
when He made me.
It was in His plans.
Now I can say
I'm childless but not by choice.
I am proud of me.
God chose me to be childless
and it is okay with me.
I am beautiful, worthy, special!
I am me!
It feels good to say these words.

Melvin Douglas Johnson

Too many legends has gone before us
left this earth too soon.
Melvin Douglas Johnson is one of them.
How do I write a poem about him
to do him justice?
It's so hard to do!
He is a phenomenal poet!
He is so loved by the poetry community!
Listen to him
you will be in awe as he reads his poetry.
Melvin is a special poet
who cares about the community.
He inspired so many poets.
He is an influencer, a mentor, a leader,
an activist, a great man.
He is kind, spreads love to all he meets.
He encourage poets to push forward.
He left a big print,
a big poetry print in this world.
Nyla's famous poem for Melvin-
"Save the Last Dance for Me."
He stands up for everyone
no matter who you are.
He stands up for justice without fear.
He is one of a kind.
He is Melvin Douglas Johnson.
He is so many things.
He should be celebrated during
The Black History Month.
Let's celebrate Melvin and his life here on earth.
Let's not leave him out.
Melvin and his poetry will live on forever
even after we're gone from this earth.

What Poetry Means to Me

Poetry to me is like
music is to a musician
stars is to the night sky.
Poetry is my passion
essence to my life
to my well-being.
I write because God gave me
this talent and I will use it.
I write because I need to,
I have something to say.
Poetry gives me support.
I love poetry whether
it's free verse or structured forms.
I hunger and thirst for poetry.

Noreen Snyder

Ramkrishna

Paul

Ramkrishna Paul

HI, I, Ramkrishna Paul, came of an ordinary peasant family. Teaching is my profession. I am working as an English teacher at a high school. Life is full of struggle undergoing hardships. Simple living, high thinking is my humble life style.

I am fond of writing poems since my childhood. Reading the same is my hobby. I like most to write in free Verse. Graduated with honors in English from a college of West honors M.A, in English in distance mode of education from a university at Salem. Now I am living in Siliguri, in the state of West Bengal, India.

Teaching is my profession but writing is my passion. Doing good to people is my religion.

Rhythm Of Spring

Spring springs after the cold
Leaving the old
With the twigs, peeping out,
Smell, oozing like nectar.
Nature looking all splendour
With her store of vast variety,
At every door far or near
Displaying all wealth, rich
In attire.
Festivals of myriad kinds
Find a lease of bliss
To please minds left astray so far,
To let the dormant joy arouse,
To let the charm, pale and faded, lost
In the mist re-appear.
Blue, serene sky smiling above
A sphere filled with gentle air
A tune of soothing song
Pervades all around
At time of flying on rosy wings
Fluttering
To the dance of dreams.

Flowers Being Trampled

Flowers in garden, a paradise on earth:
Who is not charmed to pick one
Outside the sight of the gardener?
Not unfair to have been captivated by
Their aroma, spread on all corner
For even the honeybees or butterfly.
The magical flowers displaying them
All pervading beauty, wealth and prism
Colour and shapes, fragrance and
Freedom, so liberal, hides nothing
But unveils their Self for days together
For Appeal is from the end so stronger.

Blossoms, embodiment of Innocence
And Beauty; symbol of Blissful purity
And sanctity; born for Devotion and
Bound for adoration 're being strangled
Shamelessly to have the taste of blood,
By snapping and eating up to gratify
Wolfish Greed; by banishing Humanity,
Killing His Soul, harrowing Her Chastity.

Ramkrishna Paul

Mind Not Without Fear

Where is the mind that can feel
What is good, what is ill?
Where is the mind that can see
What is fact, what is eerie?
Where is the mind that can hear
What is just, what is error?
Where is the mind that can touch
What is smooth, what is rough?
Where is the mind that can care
What is sublime, what is fair?
Where is the mind that can judge
What is straight, what is a jazz?
Where is the mind that can decide
What is life, what is suicide?
Where is the mind that can express
What is foul, what is respect?
Where is the mind that can dare
What is truth, who is a liar?
Where is the heart that doesn't hurt
The poor, honest one of earth?

Remembering

our fallen soldiers of verse

Janet Perkins Caldwell

February 14, 1959 ~ September 20, 2016

Alan W. Jankowski

16 March 1961 ~ 10 March 2017

The Butterfly Effect

"IS" in effect

Inner Child Press

News

Published Books

by

Poetry Posse Members

We are so excited to share and announce a few of the current books, as well as the new and upcoming books of some of our Poetry Posse authors.

On the following pages we present to you ...

Alicja Maria Kuberska
Jackie Davis Allen
Gail Weston Shazor
hülya n. yılmaz
Nizar Sartawi
Elizabeth E. Castillo
Faleeha Hassan
Fahredin Shehu
Kimberly Burnham
Caroline 'Ceri' Nazareno
Eliza Segiet
Teresa E. Gallion
William S. Peters, Sr.

Now Available

www.innerchildpress.com

Once upon a Time

in

Turkey

hülya n. yılmaz

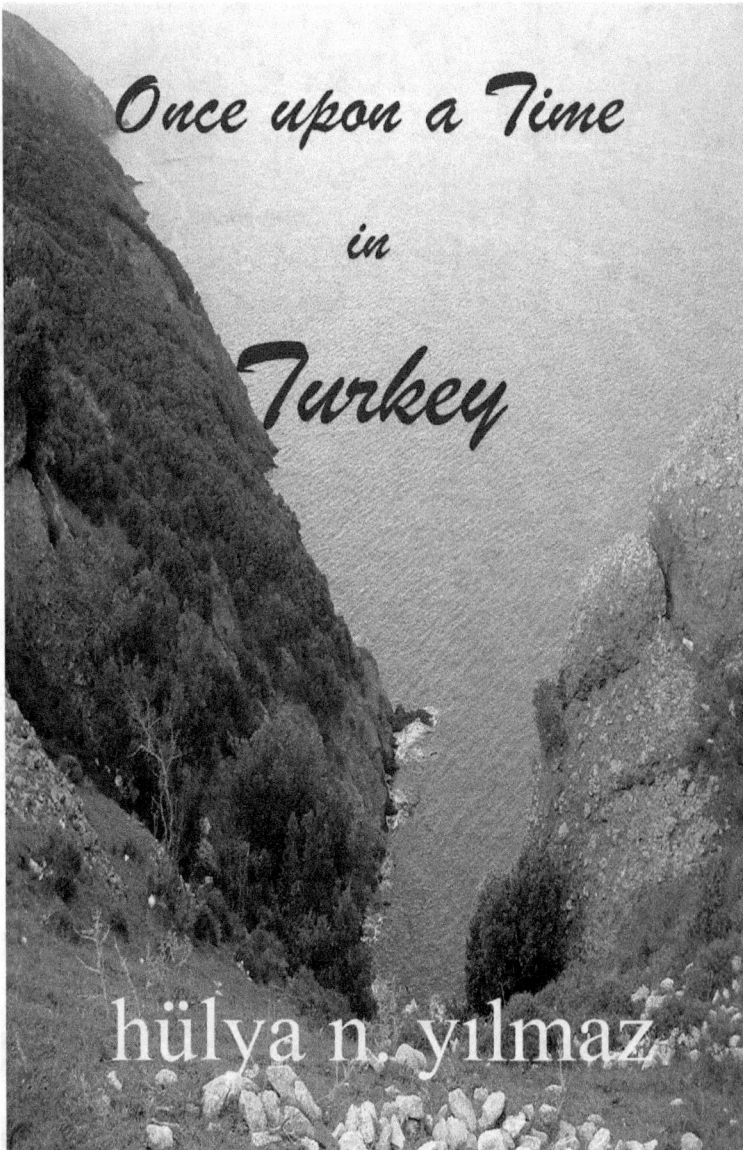

Now Available
www.innerchildpress.com

Unapologetically

BLACK

&

Blues

william s. peters, sr.

Now Available

www.innerchildpress.com

UMAMI
The Essence of Deliciousness

Fahredin Shehu

Now Available
www.innerchildpress.com

After the Frost

Alicja Maria Kuberska

Now Available

www.innerchildpress.com

153

Fahredin Shehu

O R M U S

Now Available

www.innerchildpress.com

Ahead of My Time

... from the Streets to the Stages

Albert 'Infinite' Carrasco

Eliza Segiet

To Be More

Now Available at

www.amazon.com/gp/product/B08MYL5B7S/ref=
dbs_a_def_rwt_hsch_vapi_tkin_p1_i2

SEARCH FOR THE MAGICAL MULTILINGUAL FROG

A Tale of Ribbit in 50 Languages

KIMBERLY BURNHAM

Now Available at
www.innerchildpress.com

157

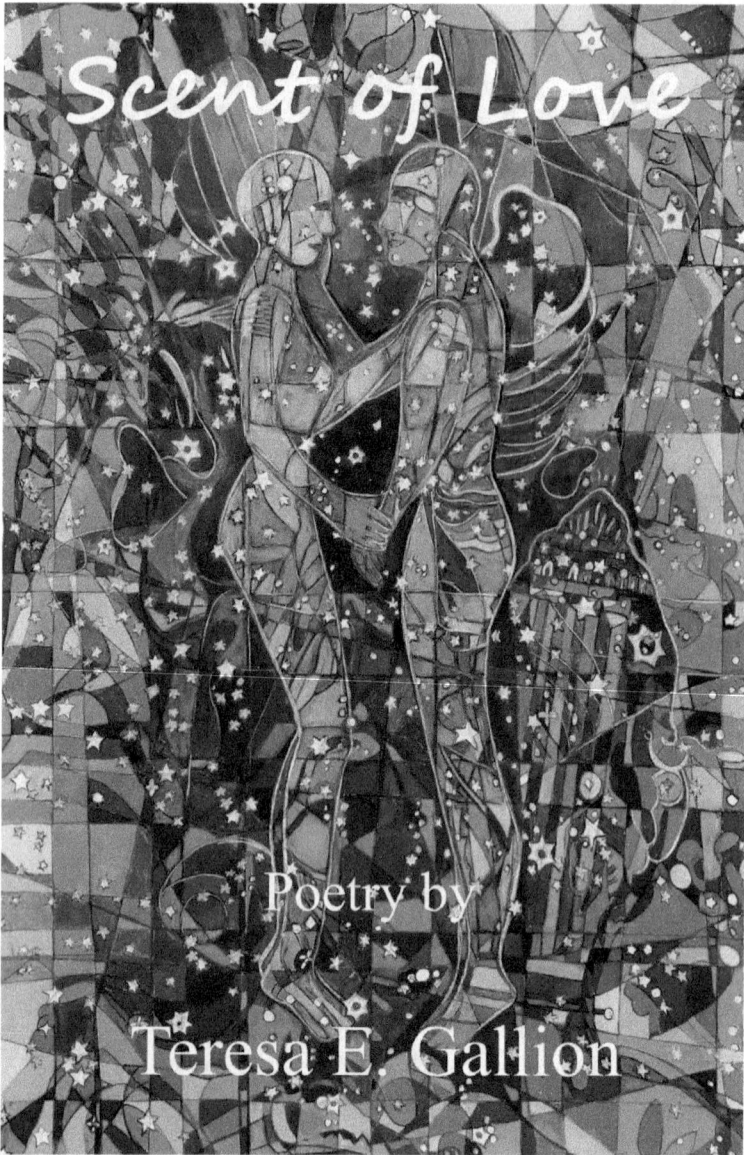

Scent of Love

Poetry by

Teresa E. Gallion

Now Available

www.innerchildpress.com

Inner Reflections
of the
Muse

Elizabeth Castillo

Now Available
www.innerchildpress.com

159

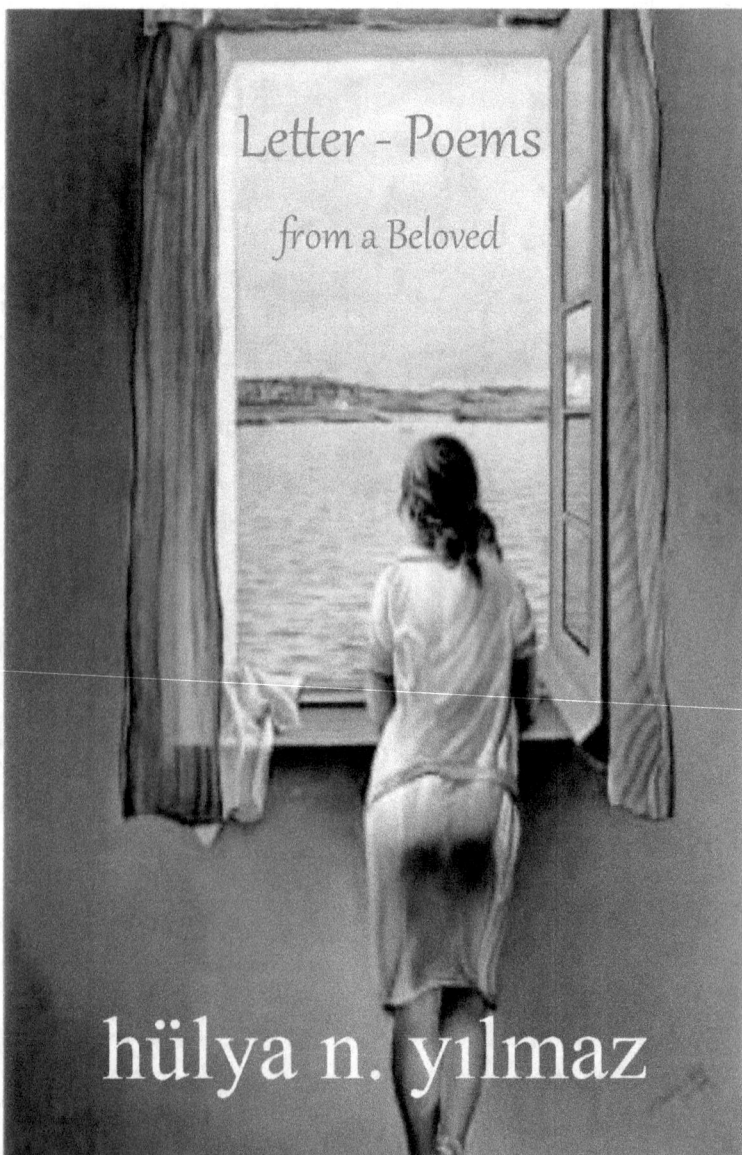

Letter - Poems

from a Beloved

hülya n. yılmaz

Now Available
www.innerchildpress.com

Now Available

www.innerchildpress.com

One Eye Open

u n i r 1.

william s. peters, sr

Now Available

www.innerchildpress.com

The Book of krisar

volume v

william s. peters, sr.

Now Available

www.innerchildpress.com

The Book of krisar

Volume I

william s. peters, sr.

The Book of krisar

Volume II

william s. peters, sr.

Now Available

www.innerchildpress.com

The Book of krisar

Volume III

william s. peters, sr.

The Book of krisar

Volume IV

william s. peters, sr.

Now Available

www.innerchildpress.com

Velvet Passions

of

Calibrated Quarks

Caroline Nazareno-Gabis

Now Available

www.innerchildpress.com

Unpaired

Eliza Segiet

Translated by Artur Komoter

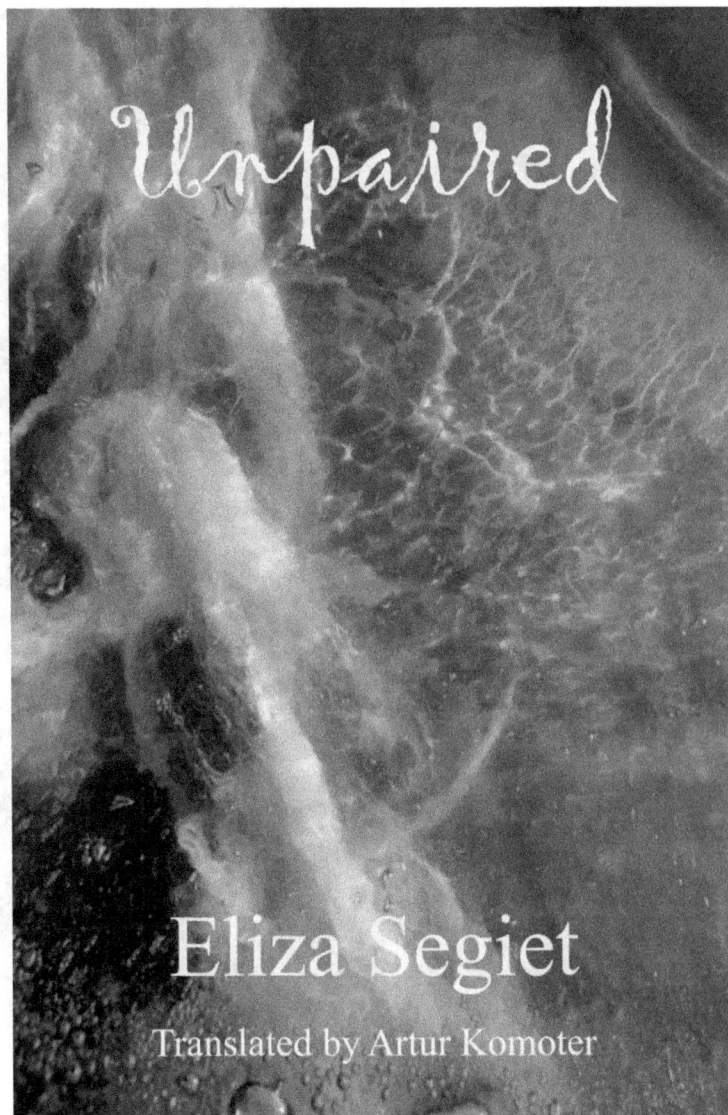

Private Issue

www.innerchildpress.com

Canlarım

My Lifeblood

poetry in Turkish and English

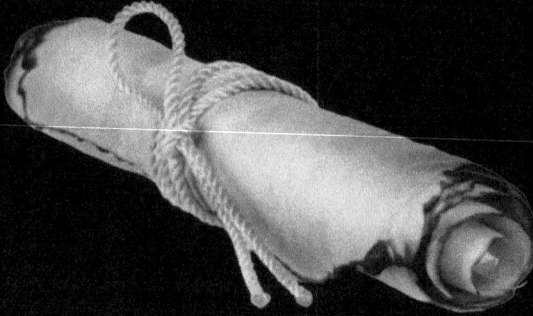

hülya n. yılmaz

Now Available

www.innerchildpress.com

Butterfly's Voice

Faleeha Hassan

Translated by William M. Hutchins

Now Available at

www.innerchildpress.com

No Illusions

Through the Looking Glass

Jackie Davis Allen

Now Available at

www.innerchildpress.com

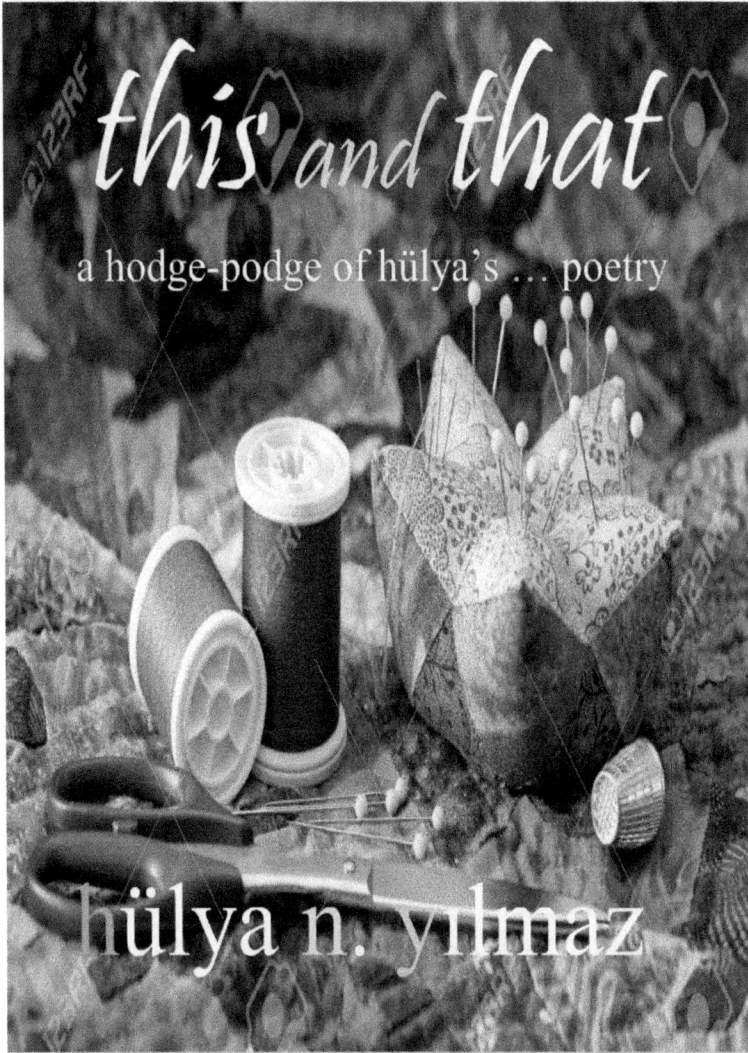

this and that

a hodge-podge of hülya's ... poetry

hülya n. yilmaz

Now Available at
www.innerchildpress.com

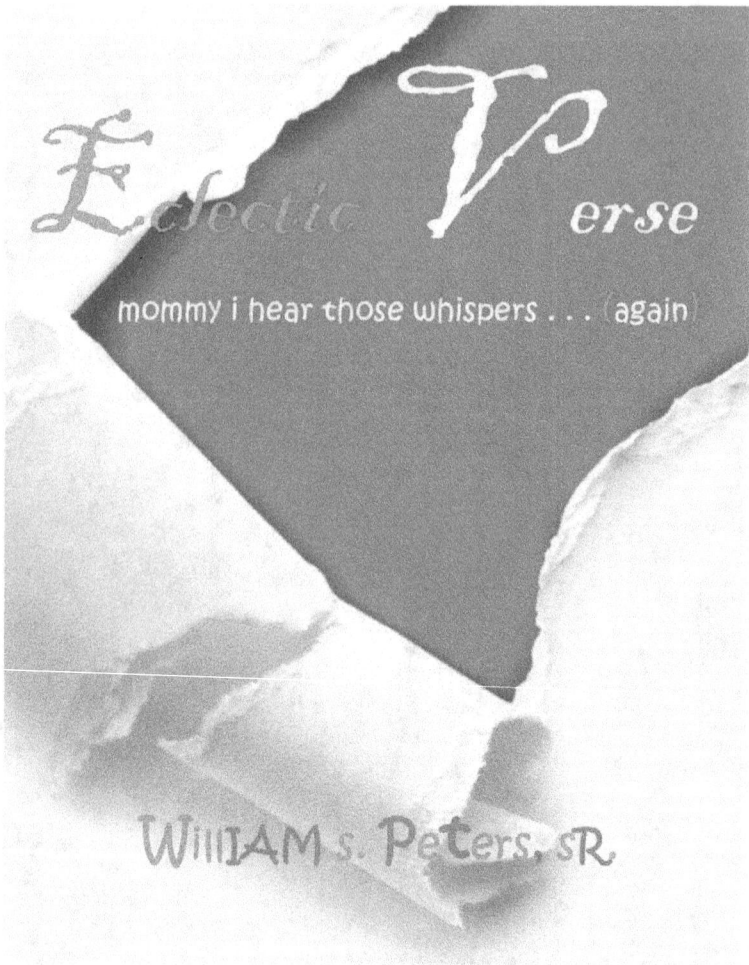

Eclectic Verse

mommy i hear those whispers . . . (again)

WilliAM s. PeTers, sR

Now Available at
www.innerchildpress.com

HERENOW

FAHREDIN SHEHU

Now Available at
www.innerchildpress.com

Magnetic People

Eliza Segiet

Translated by Artur Komoter

Now Available at
www.innerchildpress.com

Dark Side
of the
Moon

Jackie Davis Allen

Now Available at
www.innerchildpress.com

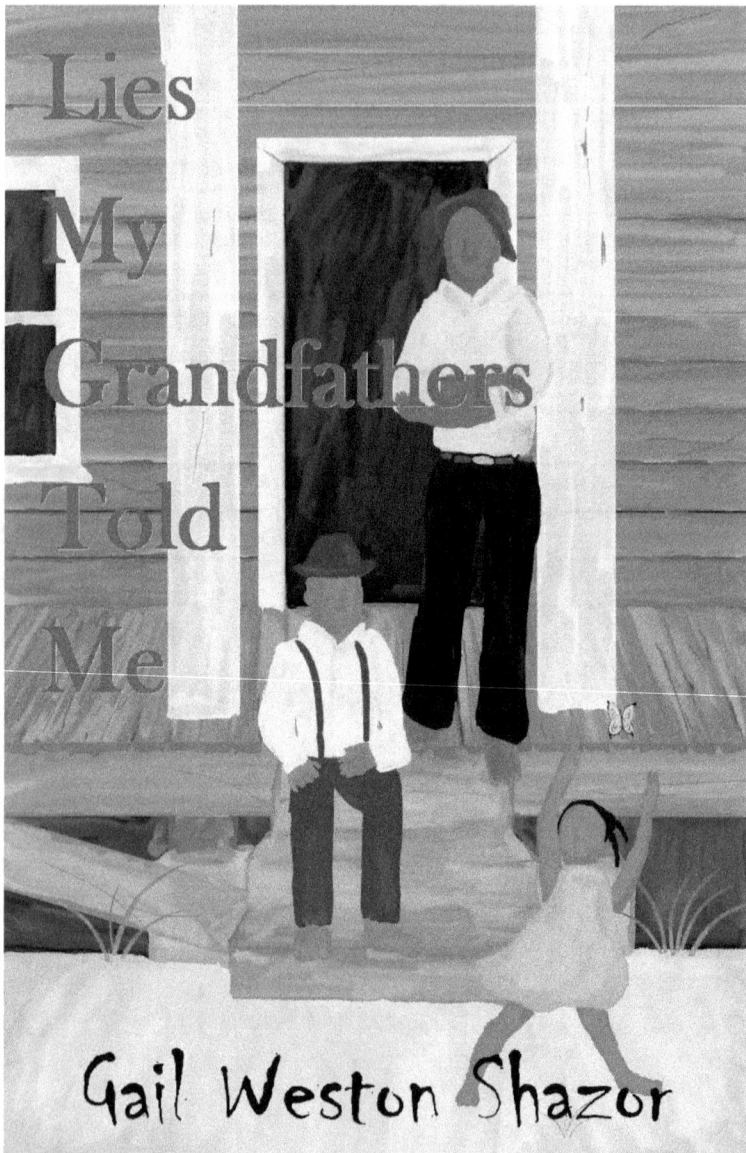

Lies My Grandfathers Told Me

Gail Weston Shazor

Now Available at
www.innerchildpress.com

Aflame

Memoirs in Verse

hülya n. yılmaz

Now Available at
www.innerchildpress.com

Mass Graves

Faleeha Hassan

Now Available at
www.innerchildpress.com

Breakfast

for

Butterflies

Faleeha Hassan

Now Available at
www.innerchildpress.com

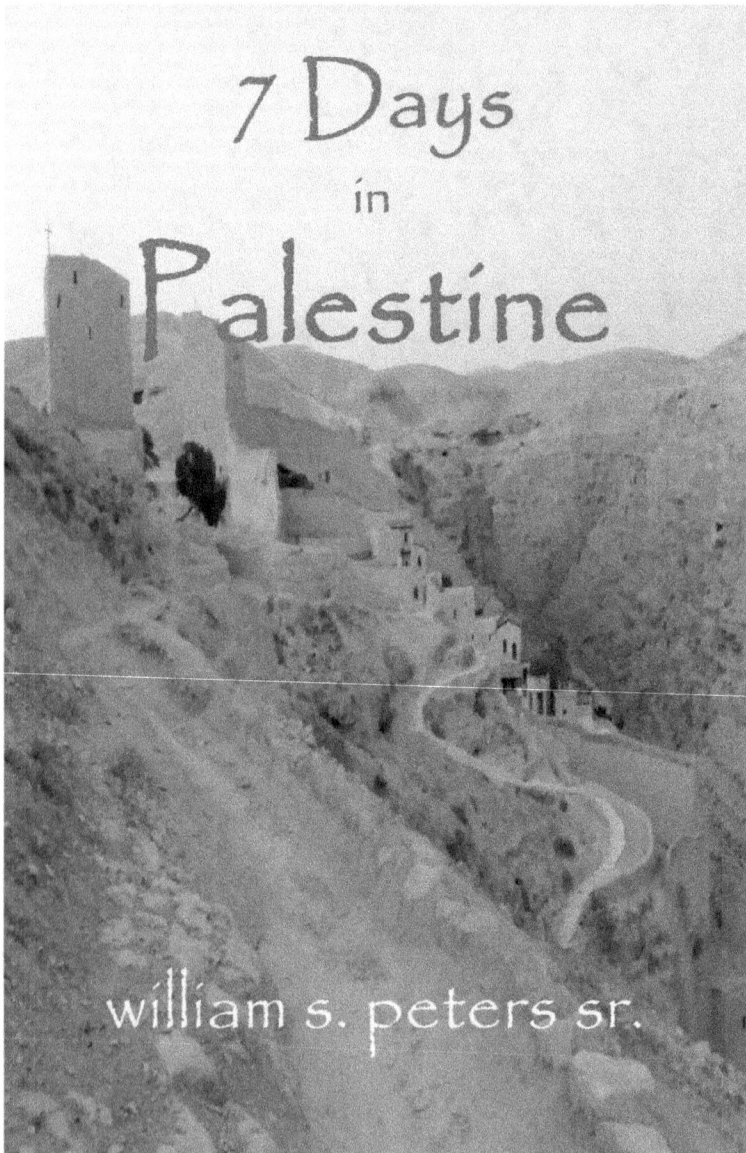

7 Days
in
Palestine

william s. peters sr.

Now Available at
www.innerchildpress.com

inner child press
presents

Tunisian Dreams

william s. peters, sr.

Now Available at
www.innerchildpress.com

INNER CHILD PRESS

THIS IS WHY I
SLEEP

william s. peters sr.

Now Available at
www.innerchildpress.com

Other

Anthological

works from

Inner Child Press International

www.innerchildpress.com

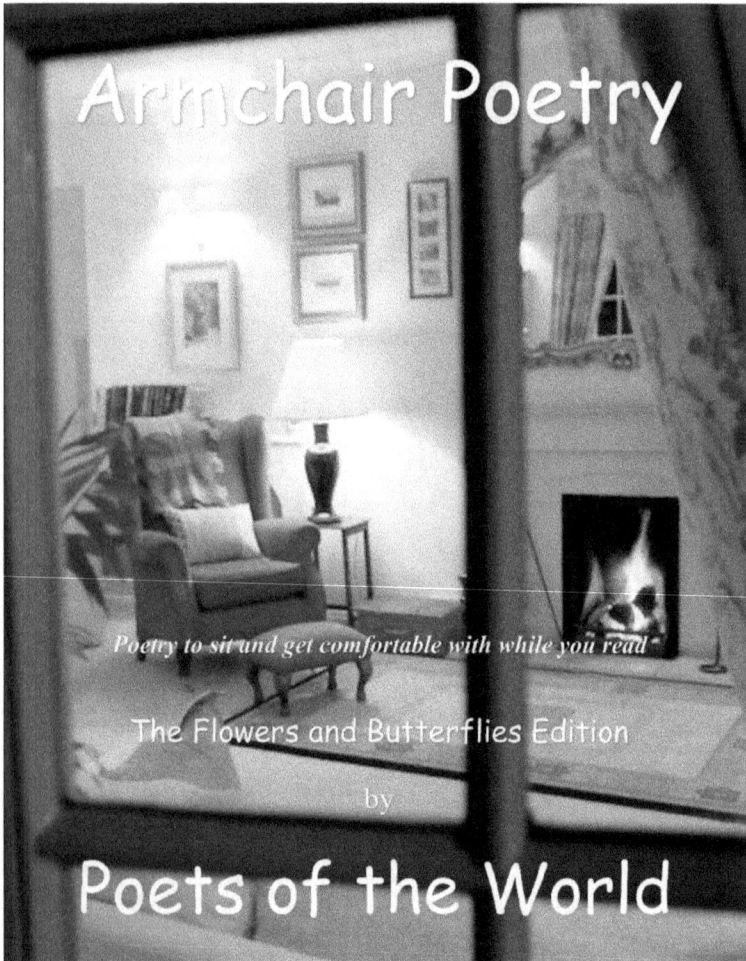

Armchair Poetry

Poetry to sit and get comfortable with while you read

The Flowers and Butterflies Edition

by

Poets of the World

Now Available

www.worldhealingworldpeacepoetry.com

Inner Child Press International
&
The Year of the Poet
present

Poetry

the best of 2022

Poets of the World

Now Available

www.worldhealingworldpeacepoetry.com

World Healing World Peace

2022

Poets for Humanity

Now Available

www.worldhealingworldpeacepoetry.com

World Healing World Peace
2020

Poets for Humanity

Now Available

www.worldhealingworldpeacepoetry.com

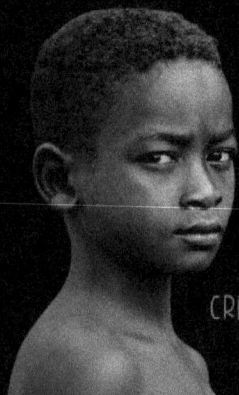

I want to
Live

an examination of Black & White issues

POETRY

ANALYSES

STORIES

CREATIVE WRITING

CRITICAL ESSAYS

WRITERS FOR HUMANITY

Now Available
www.innerchildpress.com

190

Inner Child Press International
&
The Year of the Poet
present

Poetry
the best of 2020

Poets of the World

Now Available
www.innerchildpress.com

Inner Child Press International

presents

W.A.R.

We Are Revolution

Poets for Humanity

Now Available
www.innerchildpress.com

the **H**eart of a **P**oet

words for a better tomorrow

The Conscious Poets

Now Available

www.innerchildpress.com

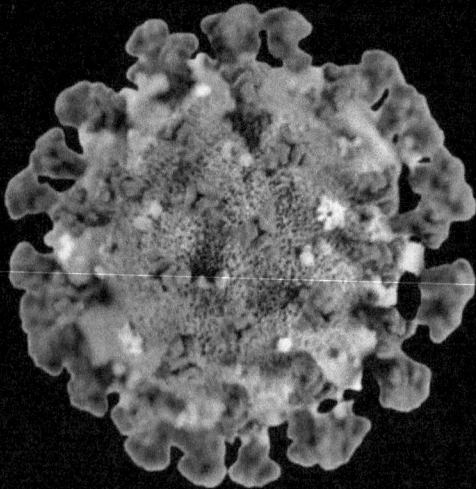

Corona

Social Distancing

Poets for Humanity

Now Available
www.innerchildpress.com

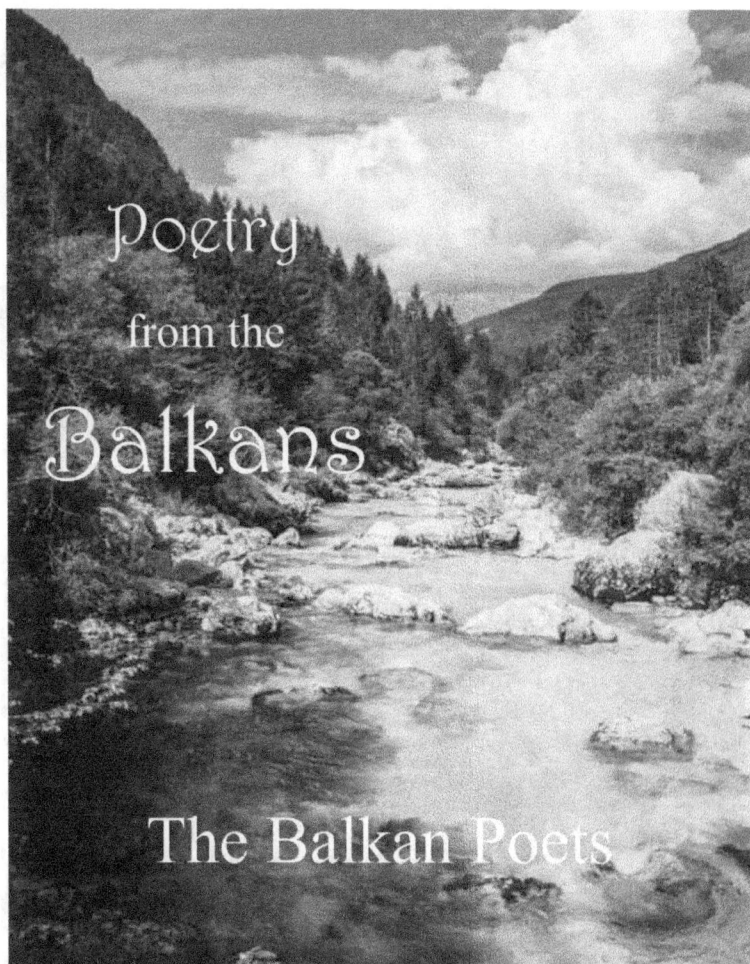

Poetry
from the
Balkans

The Balkan Poets

Now Available at
www.innerchildpress.com

Inner Child Press Anthologies

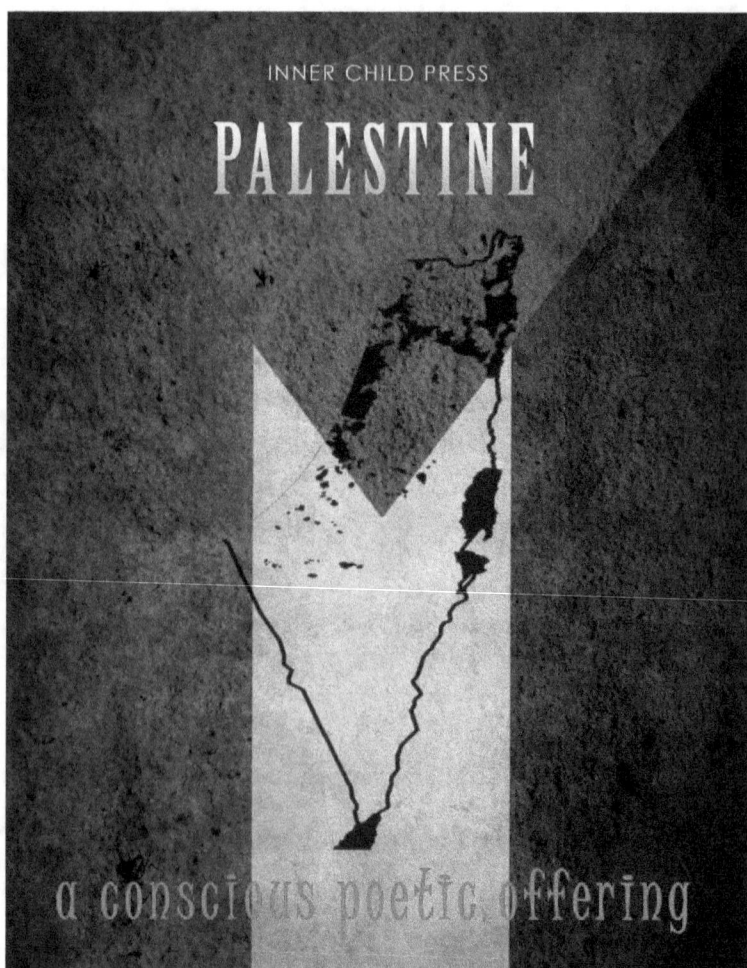

INNER CHILD PRESS

PALESTINE

a conscious poetic offering

Now Available at
www.innerchildpress.com

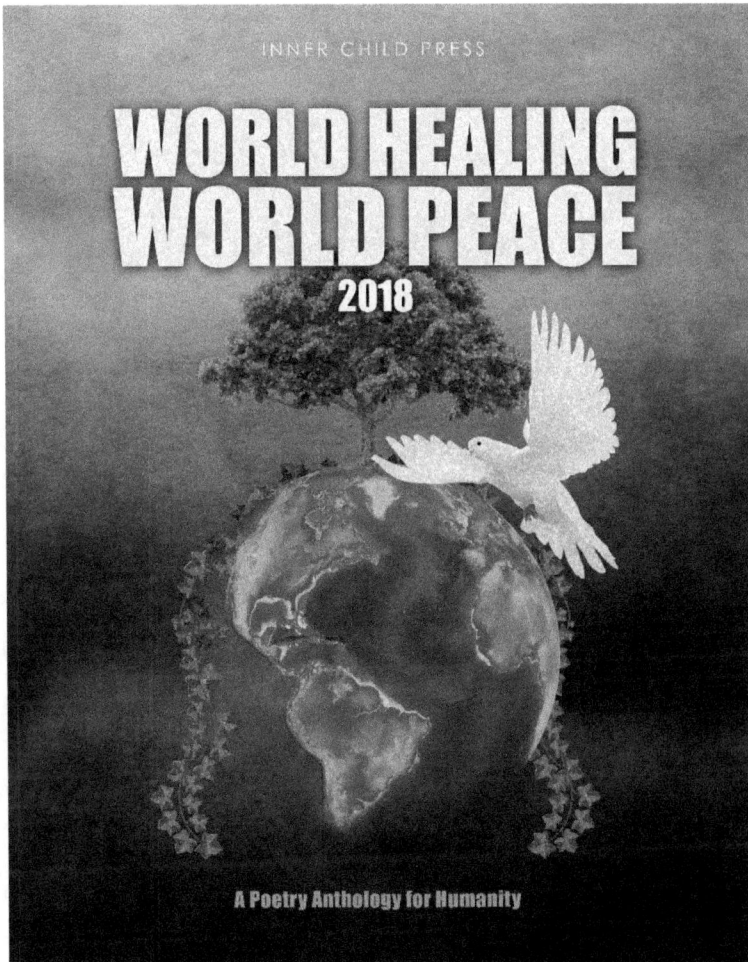

INNER CHILD PRESS

WORLD HEALING
WORLD PEACE
2018

A Poetry Anthology for Humanity

Now Available at
www.innerchildpress.com

Inner Child Press International
presents

A Love Anthology
2019

The Love Poets

Now Available
www.worldhealingworldpeacepoetry.com

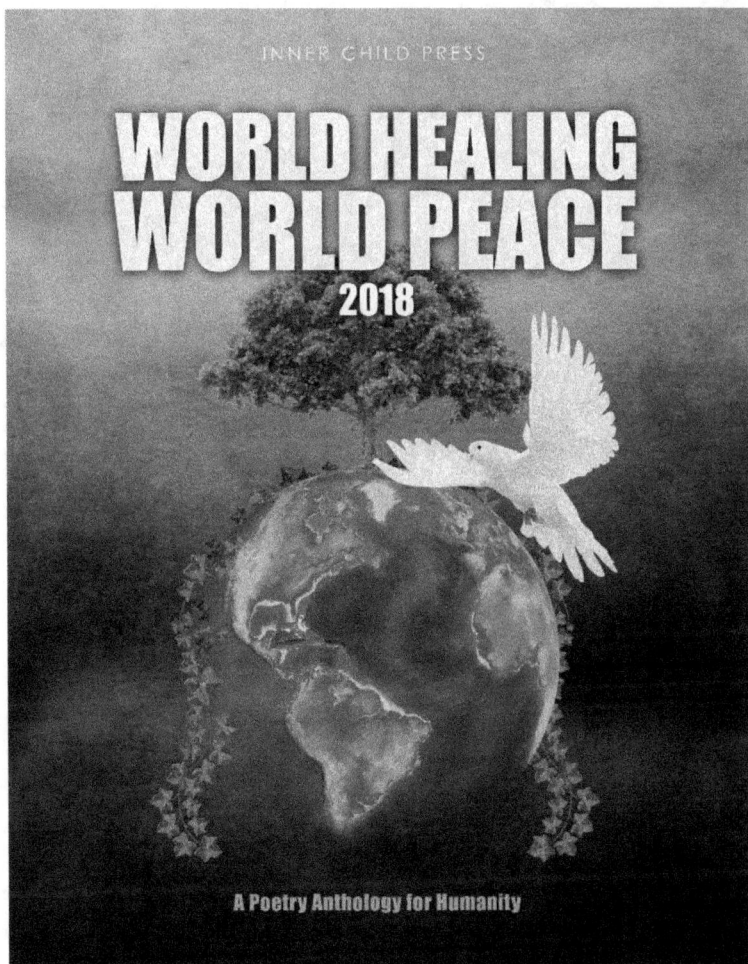

INNER CHILD PRESS

WORLD HEALING
WORLD PEACE
2018

A Poetry Anthology for Humanity

Now Available

www.worldhealingworldpeacepoetry.com

Now Available

Voices from Iraq
The Poets of Iraq

aleppo
The Conscious Writers

Dengên helbestvanên kurd ji Rojava
Kurdish Voices
A Kurdish - English Poetry Anthology

INNER CHILD PRESS
WORLD HEALING
WORLD PEACE
2016
A Poetry Anthology for Humanity

Now Available
www.innerchildpress.com/anthologies

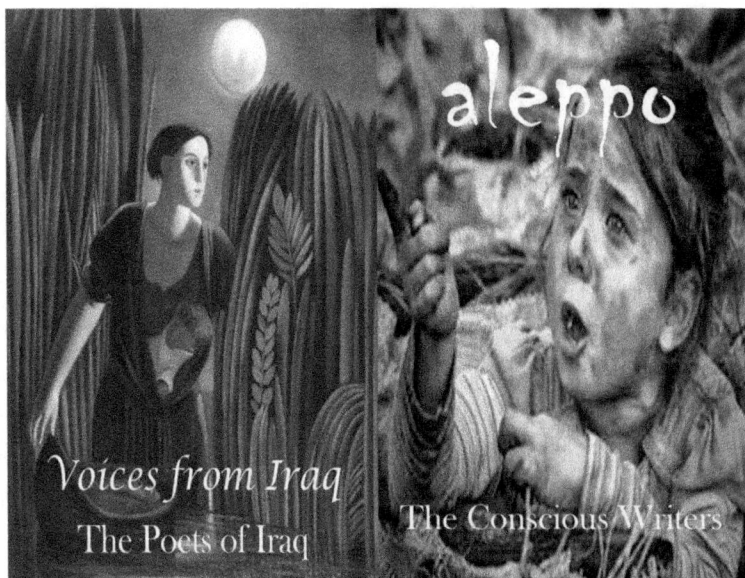

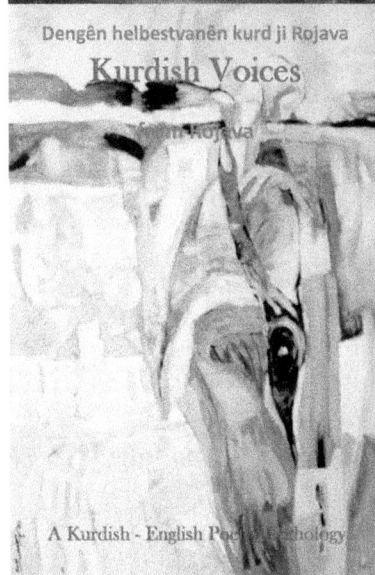

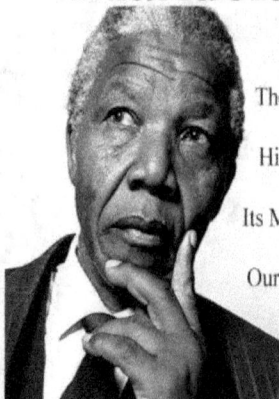

Mandela

The Man

His Life

Its Meaning

Our Words

Poetry . . . Commentary & Stories
The Anthological Writers

A GATHERING OF WORDS

POETRY & COMMENTARY
FOR
TRAYVON MARTIN

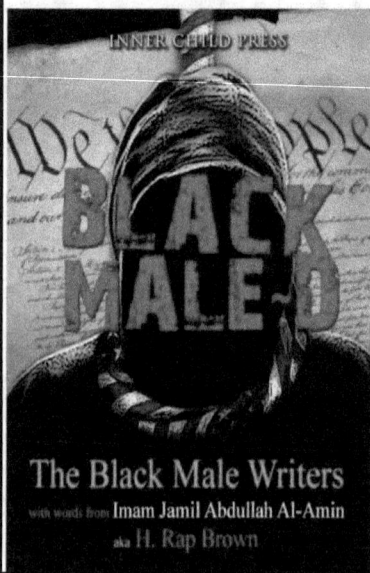

INNER CHILD PRESS

BLACK MALE-D

The Black Male Writers
with words from Imam Jamil Abdullah Al-Amin
aka H. Rap Brown

I

want

my

poetry

to . . . *volume* 4

the conscious poets

inspired by . . . Monte Smith

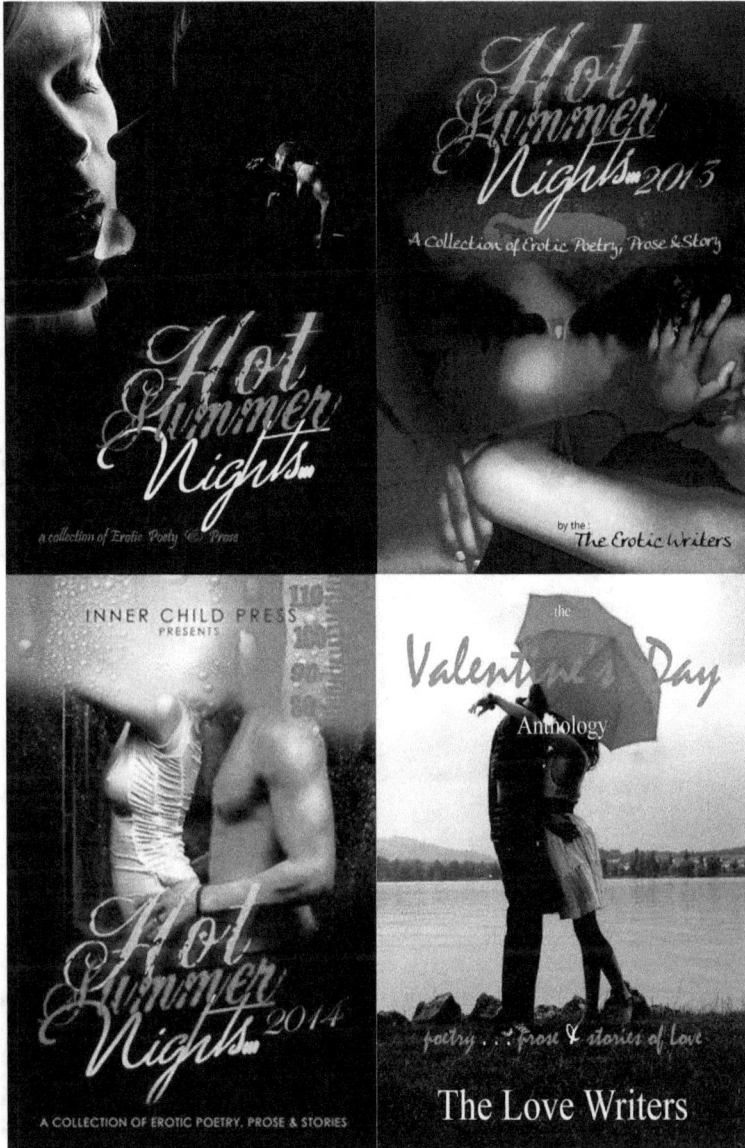

Now Available

www.innerchildpress.com/anthologies

healing through words

Poetry ... Prose ... Prayer ... Stories

Janet
gone too soon . . .

a
Poetically
Spoken
Anthology
volume 1
Collector's Edition

The Poetry Posse
Presents

an anthology
of

Love

The Poetry Posse 2016

Now Available

i
want my
PoEtRy
to . . .

a collection of the Voices of Many inspired by . . .
Monte Smith

a collection of the Voices of Many inspired by . . .
Monte Smith

i
want my
PoEtRy
to . . .
volume II

i
want
my
Poetry
to . . . volume 3

a collection of the Voices of Many inspired by . . .
Monte Smith

11 Words

(9 lines . . .)

for those who are challenged

an anthology of Poetry inspired by . . .

Poetry Dancer

Now Available
www.innerchildpress.com/anthologies

205

The Year of the Poet
January 2014

The Poetry Posse

Jamie Bond
Gail Weston Shazor
Albert 'Infinite' Carrasco
Siddartha Beth Pierce
Janet P. Caldwell
June 'Bugg' Barefield
Debbie M. Allen
Tony Henninger
Joe DaVerbal Minddancer
Robert Gibbons
Neetu Wali
Shareef Abdur-Rasheed
William S. Peters, Sr.

Carnation

Our January Feature
Terri L. Johnson

the Year of the Poet
February 2014

violets

The Poetry Posse

Jamie Bond
Gail Weston Shazor
Albert 'Infinite' Carrasco
Siddartha Beth Pierce
Janet P. Caldwell
June 'Bugg' Barefield
Debbie M. Allen
Tony Henninger
Joe DaVerbal Minddancer
Robert Gibbons
Neetu Wali
Shareef Abdur-Rasheed
William S. Peters, Sr.

Our February Features
Teresa E. Gallion & Robert Gibson

the Year of the Poet
March 2014

The Poetry Posse

Jamie Bond
Gail Weston Shazor
Albert 'Infinite' Carrasco
Siddartha Beth Pierce
Janet P. Caldwell
June 'Bugg' Barefield
Debbie M. Allen
Tony Henninger
Joe DaVerbal Minddancer
Robert Gibbons
Neetu Wali
Shareef Abdur-Rasheed
Kimberly Burnham
William S. Peters, Sr.

daffodil

Our March Featured Poets
Alicia C. Cooper & Hülya Yılmaz

the Year of the Poet
April 2014

The Poetry Posse

Jamie Bond
Gail Weston Shazor
Albert 'Infinite' Carrasco
Siddartha Beth Pierce
Janet P. Caldwell
June 'Bugg' Barefield
Debbie M. Allen
Tony Henninger
Joe DaVerbal Minddancer
Robert Gibbons
Neetu Wali
Shareef Abdur-Rasheed
Kimberly Burnham
William S. Peters, Sr.

Our April Featured Poets
Fahredin Shehu
Martina Reisz Newberry
Justin Blackburn
Monte Smith

Sweet Pea

celebrating International poetry month

Now Available
www.innerchildpress.com/the-year-of-the-poet

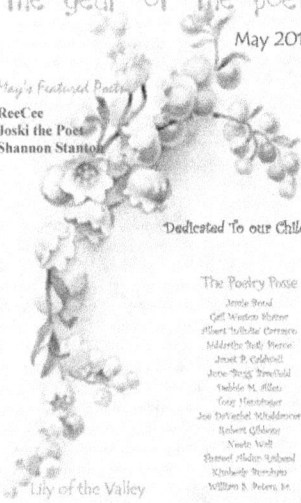

the year of the poet
May 2014

May's Featured Poets
ReeCee
Joski the Poet
Shannon Stanton

Dedicated To our Children

The Poetry Posse
Jamie Bond
Gail Weston Shazor
Albert 'Infinite' Carrasco
Siddartha Beth Pierce
Janet P. Caldwell
June 'Bugg' Barefield
Debbie M. Allen
Tony Henninger
Joe DaVerbal Minddancer
Robert Gibbons
Neetu Wali
Shareef Abdur-Rasheed
Kimberly Burnham
William S. Peters, Sr.

Lily of the Valley

the Year of the Poet
June 2014

Love & Relationship

Rose

June's Featured Poets
Shamrolie McLin
Jacqueline D. E. Kennedy
Abraham N. Benjamin

The Poetry Posse
Jamie Bond
Gail Weston Shazor
Albert 'Infinite' Carrasco
Siddartha Beth Pierce
Janet P. Caldwell
June 'Bugg' Barefield
Debbie M. Allen
Tony Henninger
Joe DaVerbal Minddancer
Robert Gibbons
Neetu Wali
Shareef Abdur-Rasheed
Kimberly Burnham
William S. Peters, Sr.

The Year of the Poet
July 2014

July Feature Poets
Christena A.V. Williams
Dr. John R. Strum
Kolade Olanrewaju Freedom

The Poetry Posse
Jamie Bond
Gail Weston Shazor
Siddartha Beth Pierce
Janet P. Caldwell
June 'Bugg' Barefield
Debbie M. Allen
Tony Henninger
Joe DaVerbal Minddancer
Robert Gibbons
Neetu Wali
Shareef Abdur-Rasheed
Kimberly Burnham
William S. Peters, Sr.

Lotus
Asian Flower of the Month

The Year of the Poet
August 2014

Gladiolus

The Poetry Posse
Jamie Bond
Gail Weston Shazor
Albert 'Infinite' Carrasco
Siddartha Beth Pierce
Janet P. Caldwell
June 'Bugg' Barefield
Debbie M. Allen
Tony Henninger
Joe DaVerbal Minddancer
Robert Gibbons
Neetu Wali
Shareef Abdur-Rasheed
Kimberly Burnham
William S. Peters, Sr.

August Feature Poets
Ann White • Rosalind Cherry • Sheila Jenkins

Now Available

www.innerchildpress.com/the-year-of-the-poet

The Year of the Poet
September 2014

Aster — Morning-Glory

Wild Chicory of September Birth of Flower

September Feature Poets
Florence Malone * Keith Alan Hamilton

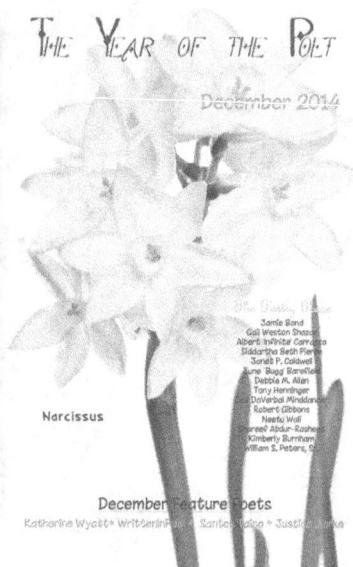

The Poetry Posse
Jamie Bond * Gail Weston Shazor * Albert Infinite Carrasco * Siddartha Beth Pierce
Janet P. Caldwell * June 'Bugg' Barefield * Debbie M. Allen * Tony Henninger
Joe DaVerbal Minddancer * Robert Gibbons * Neetu Wali * Shareef Abdur-Rasheed
Kimberly Burnham * William S. Peters, Sr.

THE YEAR OF THE POET
October 2014

Red Poppy

The Poetry Posse
Jamie Bond * Gail Weston Shazor * Albert Infinite Carrasco * Siddartha Beth Pierce
Janet P. Caldwell * June 'Bugg' Barefield * Debbie M. Allen * Tony Henninger
Joe DaVerbal Minddancer * Robert Gibbons * Neetu Wali * Shareef Abdur-Rasheed
Kimberly Burnham * William S. Peters, Sr.

October Feature Poets
Ceri Naz * Rajendra Padhi * Elizabeth Castillo

THE YEAR OF THE POET
November 2014

Chrysanthemum

The Poetry Posse
Jamie Bond * Gail Weston Shazor * Albert Infinite Carrasco * Siddartha Beth Pierce
Janet P. Caldwell * June 'Bugg' Barefield * Debbie M. Allen * Tony Henninger
Joe DaVerbal Minddancer * Robert Gibbons * Neetu Wali * Shareef Abdur-Rasheed
Kimberly Burnham * William S. Peters, Sr.

November Feature Poets
Jocelyn Mosman * Jackie Allen * James Moore * Neville Hiatt

THE YEAR OF THE POET
December 2014

Narcissus

The Poetry Posse
Jamie Bond
Gail Weston Shazor
Albert Infinite Carrasco
Siddartha Beth Pierce
Janet P. Caldwell
June 'Bugg' Barefield
Debbie M. Allen
Tony Henninger
Joe DaVerbal Minddancer
Neetu Wali
Shareef Abdur-Rasheed
Kimberly Burnham
William S. Peters, Sr.

December Feature Poets
Katharine Wyatt* WrittenInRed * Santer Judon * Justin Dunbe

Now Available
www.innerchildpress.com/the-year-of-the-poet

208

THE YEAR OF THE POET II
January 2015

Garnet

The Poetry Posse
Jamie Bond
Gail Weston Shazor
Albert 'Infinite' Carrasco
Siddartha Beth Pierce
Janet P. Caldwell
Tony Henninger
Joe DaVerbal Minddancer
Robert Gibbons
Neetu Wali
Shareef Abdur ~ Rasheed
Kimberly Burnham
Ann White
Keith Alan Hamilton
Katherine Wyatt
Fahredin Shehu
Hülya N. Yılmaz
Teresa E. Gallion
Jackie Allen
William S. Peters, Sr.

January Feature Poets
Bismay Mohanti * Jen Walls * Eric Judah

THE YEAR OF THE POET II
February 2015

Amethyst

THE POETRY POSSE
Jamie Bond
Gail Weston Shazor
Albert 'Infinite' Carrasco
Siddartha Beth Pierce
Janet P. Caldwell
Tony Henninger
Joe DaVerbal Minddancer
Robert Gibbons
Neetu Wali
Shareef Abdur ~ Rasheed
Kimberly Burnham
Ann White
Keith Alan Hamilton
Katherine Wyatt
Fahredin Shehu
Hülya N. Yılmaz
Teresa E. Gallion
Jackie Allen
William S. Peters, Sr.

FEBRUARY FEATURE POETS
Iram Fatima * Bob McNeil * Kerstin Centervall

The Year of the Poet II
March 2015

Our Featured Poets
Heung Sook * Anthony Arnold * Alicia Poland

Bloodstone

The Poetry Posse 2015
Jamie Bond * Gail Weston Shazor * Albert 'Infinite' Carrasco
Siddartha Beth Pierce * Janet P. Caldwell * Tony Henninger
Joe DaVerbal Minddancer * Neetu Wali * Shareef Abdur ~ Rasheed
Kimberly Burnham * Ann White * Keith Alan Hamilton
Katherine Wyatt * Fahredin Shehu * Hülya N. Yılmaz
Teresa E. Gallion * Jackie Allen * William S. Peters, Sr.

The Year of the Poet II
April 2015

Celebrating International Poetry Month

Our Featured Poets
Raja Williams * Dennis Ferado * Laure Charazac

Diamonds

The Poetry Posse 2015
Jamie Bond * Gail Weston Shazor * Albert 'Infinite' Carrasco
Siddartha Beth Pierce * Janet P. Caldwell * Tony Henninger
Joe DaVerbal Minddancer * Neetu Wali * Shareef Abdur ~ Rasheed
Kimberly Burnham * Ann White * Keith Alan Hamilton
Katherine Wyatt * Fahredin Shehu * Hülya N. Yılmaz
Teresa E. Gallion * Jackie Allen * William S. Peters, Sr.

Now Available
www.innerchildpress.com/the-year-of-the-poet

The Year of the Poet II
May 2015

May's Featured Poets
Geri Algeri
Akin Mosi Chimney
Anna Jakubczak

Emeralds

The Poetry Posse 2015
Jamie Bond * Gail Weston Shazor * Albert 'Infinite' Carrasco
Siddartha Beth Pierce * Janet P. Caldwell * Tony Henninger
Joe DaVerbal Minddancer * Neetu Wali * Shareef Abdur – Rasheed
Kimberly Burnham * Ann White * Keith Alan Hamilton
Katherine Wyatt * Fahredin Shehu * Hülya N. Yılmaz
Teresa E. Gallion * Jackie Allen * William S. Peters. Sr.

The Year of the Poet II
June 2015

June's Featured Poets
Aaabir Arustamyan * Yvette D. Murrell * Regina A. Walker

Pearl

The Poetry Posse 2015
Jamie Bond * Gail Weston Shazor * Albert 'Infinite' Carrasco
Siddartha Beth Pierce * Janet P. Caldwell * Tony Henninger
Joe DaVerbal Minddancer * Neetu Wali * Shareef Abdur – Rasheed
Kimberly Burnham * Ann White * Keith Alan Hamilton
Katherine Wyatt * Fahredin Shehu * Hülya N. Yılmaz
Teresa E. Gallion * Jackie Allen * William S. Peters. Sr.

The Year of the Poet II
July 2015

The Featured Poets for July 2015
Abhik Shome * Christina Neal * Robert Neal

Rubies

The Poetry Posse 2015
Jamie Bond * Gail Weston Shazor * Albert 'Infinite' Carrasco
Siddartha Beth Pierce * Janet P. Caldwell * Tony Henninger
Joe DaVerbal Minddancer * Neetu Wali * Shareef Abdur – Rasheed
Kimberly Burnham * Ann White * Keith Alan Hamilton
Katherine Wyatt * Fahredin Shehu * Hülya N. Yılmaz
Teresa E. Gallion * Jackie Allen * William S. Peters. Sr.

The Year of the Poet II
August 2015

Peridot

Featured Poets
Gayle Howell
Ann Chalasz
Christopher Schultz

The Poetry Posse 2015
Jamie Bond * Gail Weston Shazor * Albert 'Infinite' Carrasco
Siddartha Beth Pierce * Janet P. Caldwell * Tony Henninger
Joe DaVerbal Minddancer * Neetu Wali * Shareef Abdur – Rasheed
Kimberly Burnham * Ann White * Keith Alan Hamilton
Katherine Wyatt * Fahredin Shehu * Hülya N. Yılmaz
Teresa E. Gallion * Jackie Allen * William S. Peters. Sr.

Now Available
www.innerchildpress.com/the-year-of-the-poet

The Year of the Poet II

September 2015

Featured Poets
Alfreda Ghee * Lonneice Weeks Badley * Demetrios Trifiatis

Sapphires

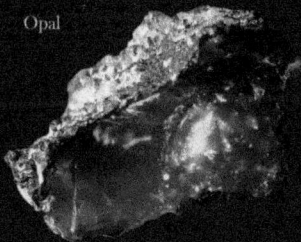

The Poetry Posse 2015
Jamie Bond * Gail Weston Shazor * Albert 'Infinite' Carrasco
Siddartha Beth Pierce * Janet P. Caldwell * Tony Henninger
Joe DaVerbal Minddancer * Neetu Wali * Shareef Abdur – Rasheed
Kimberly Burnham * Ann White * Keith Alan Hamilton
Katherine Wyatt * Fahredin Shehu * Hülya N. Yılmaz
Teresa E. Gallion * Jackie Allen * William S. Peters. Sr.

The Year of the Poet II

October 2015

Featured Poets
Monte Smith * Laura J. Wolfe * William Washington

Opal

The Poetry Posse 2015
Jamie Bond * Gail Weston Shazor * Albert 'Infinite' Carrasco
Siddartha Beth Pierce * Janet P. Caldwell * Tony Henninger
Joe DaVerbal Minddancer * Neetu Wali * Shareef Abdur – Rasheed
Kimberly Burnham * Ann White * Keith Alan Hamilton
Katherine Wyatt * Fahredin Shehu * Hülya N. Yılmaz
Teresa E. Gallion * Jackie Allen * William S. Peters, Sr.

The Year of the Poet II

November 2015

Featured Poets
Alan W. Jankowski
Bismay Mohanty
James Moore

Topaz

The Poetry Posse 2015
Jamie Bond * Gail Weston Shazor * Albert 'Infinite' Carrasco
Siddartha Beth Pierce * Janet P. Caldwell * Tony Henninger
Joe DaVerbal Minddancer * Neetu Wali * Shareef Abdur – Rasheed
Kimberly Burnham * Ann White * Keith Alan Hamilton
Katherine Wyatt * Fahredin Shehu * Hülya N. Yılmaz
Teresa E. Gallion * Jackie Allen * William S. Peters. Sr.

The Year of the Poet II

December 2015

Featured Poets
Kerione Bryan * Michelle Joan Barulich * Neville Hiatt

Turquoise

The Poetry Posse 2015
Jamie Bond * Gail Weston Shazor * Albert 'Infinite' Carrasco
Siddartha Beth Pierce * Janet P. Caldwell * Tony Henninger
Joe DaVerbal Minddancer * Neetu Wali * Shareef Abdur – Rasheed
Kimberly Burnham * Ann White * Keith Alan Hamilton
Katherine Wyatt * Fahredin Shehu * Hülya N. Yılmaz
Teresa E. Gallion * Jackie Allen * William S. Peters, Sr.

Now Available

www.innerchildpress.com/the-year-of-the-poet

Now Available
www.innerchildpress.com/the-year-of-the-poet

The Year of the Poet III
May 2016

Bob Strum
Barbara Allan
D.L. Davis

Oriole

The Year of the Poet III
June 2016

Featured Poets

Qibrije Demiri- Frangu
Naime Beqiraj
Faleeha Hassan
Bedri Zyberaj

Black Necked Stilt

The Poetry Posse 2016

The Year of the Poet III
July 2016

Featured Poets

Iram Fatima 'Ashi'
Langley Shazor
Jody Doty
Emilia T. Davis

Indigo Bunting

The Year of the Poet III
August 2016

Featured Poets

Anita Dash
Irena Jovanovic
Malgorzata Gouluda

Painted Bunting

The Poetry Posse 2016

The Poetry Posse 2016

Now Available
www.innerchildpress.com/the-year-of-the-poet

The Year of the Poet III
September 2016

Featured Poets

Simone Weber
Abhijit Sen
Eunice Barbara C. Novio

Long Billed Curle

The Poetry Posse 2016

The Year of the Poet III
October 2016

Featured Poets

Lata Joseph
Krishnamurthy
James Moore

Barn Owl

The Poetry Posse 2016

The Year of the Poet III
November 2016

Featured Poets

Rosemary Burns
Robin Ouzman Hislop
Lonneice Weeks-Badler

Northern Cardinal

The Poetry Posse 2016

The Year of the Poet III
December 2016

Featured Poets

Samih Masoud
Mountassir Aziz Bien
Abdulkadir Musa

Rough Legged Hawk

The Poetry Posse 2016

Now Available

www.innerchildpress.com/the-year-of-the-poet

214

The Year of the Poet IV
January 2017

Featured Poets

Jon Winell
Natalie Shields
Irani Fatima Ashi

Quaking Aspen

The Poetry Posse 2017

Gail Weston Shazor * Caroline Nazareno * Jhuma Mohanty
Nizar Sartawi * Jhana Jakubczak Vel Betty Adelan * Jen Walls
Joe DeVerbal Muddinncer * Shareef Abdur - Rasheed
Albert Carrasco * Kimberly Burnham * Elizabeth Castillo
Hulya N. Yılmaz * Falesha Hossen * Allen W. Jankowski
Teresa E. Gallion * Jackie Davis Allen * William S. Peters, Sr.

The Year of the Poet IV
February 2017

Featured Poets

Lin Ross
Sohkaina Falhi
Orwer Gilani

Witch Hazel

The Poetry Posse 2017

Gail Weston Shazor * Caroline Nazareno * Jhuma Mohanty
Nizar Sartawi * Jhana Jakubczak Vel Betty Adelan * Jen Walls
Joe DeVerbal Muddinncer * Shareef Abdur - Rasheed
Albert Carrasco * Kimberly Burnham * Elizabeth Castillo
Hulya N. Yılmaz * Falesha Hossen * Allen W. Jankowski
Teresa E. Gallion * Jackie Davis Allen * William S. Peters, Sr.

The Year of the Poet IV
March 2017

Featured Poets

Tremell Stevens
Francisca Ricinski
Jamil Abu Shaih

The Eastern Redbud

The Poetry Posse 2017

Gail Weston Shazor * Caroline Nazareno * Jhuma Mohanty
Teresa E. Gallion * Jhana Jakubczak Vel Betty Adelan
Joe DeVerbal Muddinncer * Shareef Abdur - Rasheed
Albert Carrasco * Kimberly Burnham * Elizabeth Castillo
Hulya N. Yılmaz * Falesha Hossen * Jackie Davis Allen
Jen Walls * Nizar Sartawi * William S. Peters, Sr.

The Year of the Poet IV
April 2017

Featured Poets

Dr. Ruchida Barman
Neptune Barman
Masood Khalaf

The Blossoming Cherry

The Poetry Posse 2017

Gail Weston Shazor * Caroline Nazareno * Jhuma Mohanty
Teresa E. Gallion * Jhana Jakubczak Vel Betty Adelan
Joe DeVerbal Muddinncer * Shareef Abdur - Rasheed
Albert Carrasco * Kimberly Burnham * Elizabeth Castillo
Hulya N. Yılmaz * Falesha Hossen * Jackie Davis Allen
Jen Walls * Nizar Sartawi * William S. Peters, Sr.

Now Available

www.innerchildpress.com/the-year-of-the-poet

The Year of the Poet IV
May 2017

The Flowering Dogwood Tree

Featured Poets
Kallisa Powell
Alicja Maria Kuberska
Fethi Sassi

The Poetry Posse 2017

Gail Weston Shazor * Caroline Nazareno * Hülya Malmatçı
Teresa E. Gallion * Jhon Jakubczak Val Betty Aldelo
Joe DaVerbal Minddancer * Shareef Abdur – Rasheed
Albert Carrasco * Kimberly Burnham * Elizabeth Castillo
Hülya N. Yılmaz * Falosha Hassen * Jackie Davis Allen
Jan Wells * Neza Sartowi * * William S. Peters, Sr.

The Year of the Poet IV
June 2017

Featured Poets
Eliza Segiet
Tzc-Min Tsai
Abdolla Issa

The Linden Tree

The Poetry Posse 2017

Hülya N. Yılmaz
Jan Wells * Neza Sartowi * William S. Peters,

The Year of the Poet IV
July 2017

Featured Poets
Anca Mihaela Bruma
Ibáa Ismail
Zvonko Taneski

The Oak Moon

The Poetry Posse 2017

The Year of the Poet IV
August 2017

Featured Poets
Jonathan Aquino
Kitty Hsu
Langley Shazor

The Hazelnut Tree

The Poetry Posse 2017

Gail Weston Shazor * Caroline Nazareno *
Teresa E. Gallion * Jhon Jakubczak Val Betty Aldelo
Joe DaVerbal Minddancer * Shareef Abdur – Rasheed
Albert Carrasco * Kimberly Burnham * Elizabeth Castillo
Hülya N. Yılmaz * Falosha Hassen * Jackie Davis Allen
Jan Wells * Neza Sartowi * * William S. Peters, Sr.

Now Available
www.innerchildpress.com/the-year-of-the-poet

216

The Year of the Poet IV
September 2017

Featured Poets

Martina Reisz Newberry
Ameer Nassir
Christine Fulco Neal
Robert Neal

The Elm Tree

The Poetry Posse 2017

Gail Weston Shazor * Caroline Nazareno * Bismay Mohanty
Teresa E. Gallion * Anna Jakubczak Vel Ratty Adalan
Joe DaVerbal Minddancer * Shareef Abdur – Rasheed
Albert Carrasco * Kimberly Burnham * Elizabeth Castillo
Hülya N. Yılmaz * Faleeha Hassan * Jackie Davis Allen
Jen Walls * Nizar Sartawi * * William S. Peters, Sr.

The Year of the Poet IV
October 2017

Featured Poets

Ahmed Abu Saleem
Nedal Al-Qaeim
Sadeddin Shahin

The Black Walnut Tree

The Poetry Posse 2017

Gail Weston Shazor * Caroline Nazareno * Bismay Mohanty
Teresa E. Gallion * Anna Jakubczak Vel Ratty Adalan
Joe DaVerbal Minddancer * Shareef Abdur – Rasheed
Albert Carrasco * Kimberly Burnham * Elizabeth Castillo
Hülya N. Yılmaz * Faleeha Hassan * Jackie Davis Allen
Jen Walls * Nizar Sartawi * * William S. Peters, Sr.

The Year of the Poet IV
November 2017

Featured Poets

Kay Peters
Alfreda D. Ghee
Gabriella Garofalo
Rosemary Cappello

The Tree of Life

The Poetry Posse 2017

Gail Weston Shazor * Caroline Nazareno * Bismay Mohanty
Teresa E. Gallion * Anna Jakubczak Vel Ratty Adalan
Joe DaVerbal Minddancer * Shareef Abdur – Rasheed
Albert Carrasco * Kimberly Burnham * Elizabeth Castillo
Hülya N. Yılmaz * Faleeha Hassan * Jackie Davis Allen
Jen Walls * Nizar Sartawi * William S. Peters, Sr.

The Year of the Poet IV
December 2017

Featured Poets

Justice Clarke
Mariel M. Pabroa
Kiley Brown

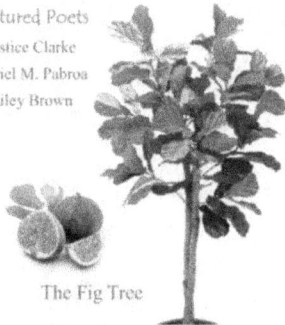

The Fig Tree

The Poetry Posse 2017

Gail Weston Shazor * Caroline Nazareno * Bismay Mohanty
Teresa E. Gallion * Anna Jakubczak Vel Ratty Adalan
Joe DaVerbal Minddancer * Shareef Abdur – Rasheed
Albert Carrasco * Kimberly Burnham * Elizabeth Castillo
Hülya N. Yılmaz * Faleeha Hassan * Jackie Davis Allen
Jen Walls * Nizar Sartawi * William S. Peters, Sr.

Now Available

www.innerchildpress.com/the-year-of-the-poet

The Year of the Poet V
January 2018
Featured Poets
Iyad Shamasnah
Yasmeen Hamzeh
Ali Abdolrezaei

Aksum

The Poetry Posse 2018
Gail Weston Shazor * Caroline Nazareno * Tezmin Ition Tsai
Hülya N. Yılmaz * Faleeha Hassan * Jackie Davis Allen
Teresa E. Gallion * Anna Jakubczak Vel Ratty Adalan
Alicja Maria Kubenska * Shareef Abdur – Rasheed
Kimberly Burnham * Elizabeth Castillo
Nizar Sartawi * William S. Peters, Sr.

The Year of the Poet V
February 2018

Sabean

Featured Poets
Muhammad Azram
Anna Szawracka
Abhilipsa Kuanar
Aanika Aery

The Poetry Posse 2018
Gail Weston Shazor * Caroline Nazareno * Tezmin Ition Tsai
Hülya N. Yılmaz * Faleeha Hassan * Jackie Davis Allen
Teresa E. Gallion * Anna Jakubczak Vel Ratty Adalan
Alicja Maria Kubenska * Shareef Abdur – Rasheed
Kimberly Burnham * Elizabeth Castillo
Nizar Sartawi * William S. Peters, Sr.

The Year of the Poet V
March 2018

Featured Poets
Iram Fatima 'Ashi'
Cassandra Swan
Jaleel Khazaal
Shazia Zaman

Mexico Cuba

Caribbean
&
Middle America

The Poetry Posse 2018
Gail Weston Shazor * Nizar Sartawi * Hülya N. Yılmaz
Jackie Davis Allen * Caroline 'Ceri' Nazareno
Alicja Maria Kubenska * Teresa E. Gallion
Faleeha Hassan * Shareef Abdur – Rasheed
Kimberly Burnham * Elizabeth Castillo
Tezmin Ition Tsai * William S. Peters. Sr.

The Year of the Poet V
April 2018

Featured Poets

The Nez Perce

The Poetry Posse 2018

Now Available
www.innerchildpress.com/the-year-of-the-poet

The Year of the Poet V
May 2018

Featured Poets

Zaddy Carreon de Leon Jr.
Sylwia K. Malinowska
Emilia Altrucci
Ofelia Prodan

The Sumerians

The Poetry Posse 2018

Gail Weston Shazor * Nizar Sartawi * Hülya N. Yılmaz
Jackie Davis Allen * Caroline 'Ceri' Nazareno
Alicja Maria Kuberska * Teresa E. Gallion
Kimberly Burnham * Shareef Abdur – Rasheed
Faleeha Hassan * Elizabeth Castillo * Swapna Behera
Tezmin Ition Tsai * William S. Peters, Sr.

The Year of the Poet V
June 2018

Featured Poets

Bilall Maliqi * Daim Miftari * Gojko Bozovic * Sofija Zivkovic

The Paleo Indians

The Poetry Posse 2018

The Year of the Poet V
July 2018

Featured Poets

Fathmah Dougani-Eddy
Mohammad Ikbal Hash
Eliza Segiet
Tom Higgins

Oceania

The Poetry Posse 2018

The Year of the Poet V
August 2018

Featured Poets

Hussein Habasch * Mircea Dan Duta * Naida Mujkić * Swagat Das

The Lapita

The Poetry Posse 2018

Gail Weston Shazor * Nizar Sartawi * Hülya N. Yılmaz
Jackie Davis Allen * Caroline 'Ceri' Nazareno
Alicja Maria Kuberska * Teresa E. Gallion
Kimberly Burnham * Shareef Abdur – Rasheed
Ashok K. Bhargava * Elizabeth Castillo * Swapna Behaera
Tezmin Ition Tsai * William S. Peters, Sr.

Now Available
www.innerchildpress.com/the-year-of-the-poet

The Year of the Poet VI
January 2019

Indigenous North Americans

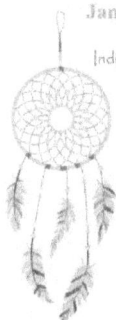

Featured Poets

Houda Elfchtali
Anthony Briscoe
Iram Fatima 'Ashi'
Dr. K. K. Mathew

Dream Catcher

The Poetry Posse 2019

Gail Weston Shazor * Joe Paire * Hülya N. Yilmaz
Jackie Davis Allen * Caroline Cerv Nazareno
Alicja Maria Kubenska * Teresa E. Gallion
Kimberly Burnham * Shareef Abdur – Rasheed
Ashok K. Bhargava * Elizabeth Castillo * Swapna Behera
Tezmin Ition Tsai * William S. Peters, Sr.

The Year of the Poet VI
February 2019

Featured Poets
Marek Łukaszewicz * Bharati Nayak
Aida G. Roque * Jean-Jacques Fournier

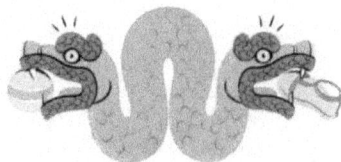

Meso-America

The Poetry Posse 2019

Gail Weston Shazor * Albert Caranco * Hülya N. Yilmaz
Jackie Davis Allen * Caroline Nazareno * Eliza Segiet
Alicja Maria Kubenska * Teresa E. Gallion * Joe Paire
Kimberly Burnham * Shareef Abdur – Rasheed
Ashok K. Bhargava * Elizabeth Castillo * Swapna Behera
Tezmin Ition Tsai * William S. Peters, Sr.

The Year of the Poet VI
March 2019

Featured Poets
Enesa Mahmic * Sybera K. Malinowska
Shurouk Hammoud * Anwer Ghani

The Caribbean

The Poetry Posse 2019

Gail Weston Shazor * Albert Carrasco * Hülya N. Yilmaz
Jackie Davis Allen * Caroline Nazareno * Eliza Segiet
Alicja Maria Kubenska * Teresa E. Gallion * Joe Paire
Kimberly Burnham * Shareef Abdur – Rasheed
Ashok K. Bhargava * Elizabeth Castillo * Swapna Behera
Tezmin Ition Tsai * William S. Peters, Sr.

The Year of the Poet VI
April 2019

Featured Poets
DL Davis * Michelle Joan Barulich
Lulëzim Haziri * Faleeha Hassan

Central & West Africa

The Poetry Posse 2019

Gail Weston Shazor * Albert Carrasco * Hülya N. Yilmaz
Jackie Davis Allen * Caroline Nazareno * Eliza Segiet
Alicja Maria Kubenska * Teresa E. Gallion * Joe Paire
Kimberly Burnham * Shareef Abdur – Rasheed
Ashok K. Bhargava * Elizabeth Castillo * Swapna Behera
Tezmin Ition Tsai * William S. Peters, Sr.

Now Available
www.innerchildpress.com/the-year-of-the-poet

221

The Year of the Poet VI
May 2019

Featured Poets

Emad Al-Haydary * Hussein Nasser Jabr
Wahab Sheriff * Abdal Razzaq Al Ameeri

Asia Southeast Asia and Maritime Asia

The Poetry Posse 2019

Gail Weston Shazor * Albert Carrasco * Hülya N. Yılmaz
Jackie Davis Allen * Caroline Nazareno * Eliza Segiet
Alicja Maria Kuberska * Teresa E. Gallion * Joe Paire
Kimberly Burnham * Shareef Abdur – Rasheed
Ashok K. Bhargava * Elizabeth Castillo * Swapna Behera
Tezmin Ition Tsai * William S. Peters, Sr.

The Year of the Poet VI
June 2019

Featured Poets

Kate Gaudi Powiekszone * Sahaj Sabharwal
Iwu Jeff * Mohamed Abdel Aziz Shmeis

Arctic
Circumpolar

The Poetry Posse 2019

Gail Weston Shazor * Albert Carrasco * Hülya N. Yılmaz
Jackie Davis Allen * Caroline Nazareno * Eliza Segiet
Alicja Maria Kuberska * Teresa E. Gallion * Joe Paire
Kimberly Burnham * Shareef Abdur – Rasheed
Ashok K. Bhargava * Elizabeth Castillo * Swapna Behera
Tezmin Ition Tsai * William S. Peters, Sr.

The Year of the Poet VI
July 2019

Featured Poets

Najiuddin Shahin * Andy Stott
Fahmida Shelai * Alok Kumar Ray

The Horn of Africa

Ethiopia   Djibouti

Somalia   Eritrea

The Poetry Posse 2019

Gail Weston Shazor * Albert Carrasco * Hülya N. Yılmaz
Jackie Davis Allen * Caroline Nazareno * Eliza Segiet
Alicja Maria Kuberska * Teresa E. Gallion * Joe Paire
Kimberly Burnham * Shareef Abdur – Rasheed
Ashok K. Bhargava * Elizabeth Castillo * Swapna Behera
Tezmin Ition Tsai * William S. Peters, Sr.

The Year of the Poet VI
August 2019

Featured Poets

Shola Balogun * Bharati Nayak
Monalisa Dash Dwibedy * Mbizo Chirasha

COEXIST

Southwest Asia

The Poetry Posse 2019

Gail Weston Shazor * Albert Carrasco * Hülya N. Yılmaz
Jackie Davis Allen * Caroline Nazareno * Eliza Segiet
Alicja Maria Kuberska * Teresa E. Gallion * Joe Paire
Kimberly Burnham * Shareef Abdur – Rasheed
Ashok K. Bhargava * Elizabeth Castillo * Swapna Behera
Tezmin Ition Tsai * William S. Peters, Sr.

Now Available

www.innerchildpress.com/the-year-of-the-poet

The Year of the Poet VI
September 2019
Featured Poets
Elena Liliana Popescu * Gobinda Biswas
Jram Fatima "Asbi" * Joseph S. Spence, Sr.
The Caucasus
The Poetry Posse 2019

The Year of the Poet VI
October 2019
Featured Poets
Segun Olivia Osuona * Denisa Kondic
Pankhuri Sinha * Christena AV Williams
The Nile Valley
The Poetry Posse 2019

The Year of the Poet VI
November 2019
Featured Poets
Rozalie Alphonsedrova * Orbindu Ganga
Smruti Ranjan Mohanty * Sofia Skleida
Northern Asia
The Poetry Posse 2019

The Year of the Poet VI
December 2019
Featured Poets
Oceania
The Poetry Posse 2019

Now Available

www.innerchildpress.com/the-year-of-the-poet

The Year of the Poet VII
January 2020

Featured Poets

H S Tyagi * Ashok Chakravarthy Tholana
Andy Scott * Anwer Ghani

1901 Jean Henry Dunant and Frédéric Passy

The Year of Peace
Celebrating past Nobel Peace Prize Recipients

The Poetry Posse 2020

Gail Weston Shazor * Albert Carasco * Hülya N. Yılmaz
Jackie Davis Allen * Caroline Nazareno * Eliza Segiet
Alicja Maria Kuberska * Teresa E. Gallion * Joe Paire
Kimberly Burnham * Shareef Abdur – Rasheed
Ashok K. Bhargava * Elizabeth Castillo * Swapna Behera
Tezmin Ition Tsai * William S. Peters, Sr.

The Year of the Poet VII
February 2020

Featured Poets

Jennifer Ades * Martina Reisz Newberry
Ibrahim Honjo * Claudia Piccinno

Henri La Fontaine ~ 1913

The Year of Peace
Celebrating past Nobel Peace Prize Recipients

The Poetry Posse 2020

Gail Weston Shazor * Albert Carasco * Hülya N. Yılmaz
Jackie Davis Allen * Caroline Nazareno * Eliza Segiet
Alicja Maria Kuberska * Teresa E. Gallion * Joe Paire
Kimberly Burnham * Shareef Abdur – Rasheed
Ashok K. Bhargava * Elizabeth Castillo * Swapna Behera
Tezmin Ition Tsai * William S. Peters, Sr.

The Year of the Poet VII
March 2020

Featured Poets

Aziz Mountassir * Krishna Paraisa
Hansie Rouweler * Rozalia Aleksandrova

Aristide Briand ~ 1926 ~ Gustav Stresemann

The Year of Peace
Celebrating past Nobel Peace Prize Recipients

The Poetry Posse 2020

Gail Weston Shazor * Albert Carasco * Hülya N. Yılmaz
Jackie Davis Allen * Caroline Nazareno * Eliza Segiet
Alicja Maria Kuberska * Teresa E. Gallion * Joe Paire
Kimberly Burnham * Shareef Abdur – Rasheed
Ashok K. Bhargava * Elizabeth Castillo * Swapna Behera
Tezmin Ition Tsai * William S. Peters, Sr.

The Year of the Poet VII
April 2020

Featured Poets

Rohini Behera * Mircea Dan Duta
Monalisa Dash Dwibedy * NilavroNill Shoovro

Carlos Saavedra Lamas ~ 1936

The Year of Peace
Celebrating past Nobel Peace Prize Recipients

The Poetry Posse 2020

Gail Weston Shazor * Albert Carasco * Hülya N. Yılmaz
Jackie Davis Allen * Caroline Nazareno * Eliza Segiet
Alicja Maria Kuberska * Teresa E. Gallion * Joe Paire
Kimberly Burnham * Shareef Abdur – Rasheed
Ashok K. Bhargava * Elizabeth Castillo * Swapna Behera
Tezmin Ition Tsai * William S. Peters, Sr.

Now Available

www.innerchildpress.com/the-year-of-the-poet

The Year of the Poet VII
May 2020
Featured Poets
Alok Kumar Ray * Eden S. Trinidad
Franco Barbato * Izabela Zubko

Ralph Bunche ~ 1950

The Year of Peace
Celebrating past Nobel Peace Prize Recipients

The Poetry Posse 2020
Gail Weston Shazor * Albert Carasco * Hülya N. Yılmaz
Jackie Davis Allen * Caroline Nazareno * Eliza Segiet
Alicja Maria Kuberska * Teresa E. Gallion * Joe Paire
Kimberly Burnham * Shareef Abdur – Rasheed
Ashok K. Bhargava * Elizabeth Castillo * Swapna Behera
Tezmin Ition Tsai * William S. Peters, Sr.

The Year of the Poet VII
June 2020
Featured Poets
Eftichia Kapardeli * Metin Cengiz
Hussein Habasch * Kosh K Mathew

Albert John Lutuli ~ 1960

The Year of Peace
Celebrating past Nobel Peace Prize Recipients

The Poetry Posse 2020
Gail Weston Shazor * Albert Carasco * Hülya N. Yılmaz
Jackie Davis Allen * Caroline Nazareno * Eliza Segiet
Alicja Maria Kuberska * Teresa E. Gallion * Joe Paire
Kimberly Burnham * Shareef Abdur – Rasheed
Ashok K. Bhargava * Elizabeth Castillo * Swapna Behera
Tezmin Ition Tsai * William S. Peters, Sr.

The Year of the Poet VII
July 2020
Featured Poets
Mykola Martyniuk * Orbindu Ganga
Roula Pollard * Karn Praktisha

Norman Ernest Borlaug ~ 1970

The Year of Peace
Celebrating past Nobel Peace Prize Recipients

The Poetry Posse 2020
Gail Weston Shazor * Albert Carasco * Hülya N. Yılmaz
Jackie Davis Allen * Caroline Nazareno * Eliza Segiet
Alicja Maria Kuberska * Teresa E. Gallion * Joe Paire
Kimberly Burnham * Shareef Abdur – Rasheed
Ashok K. Bhargava * Elizabeth Castillo * Swapna Behera
Tezmin Ition Tsai * William S. Peters, Sr.

The Year of the Poet VII
August 2020
Featured Poets
Dr Pragya Suman * Chinh Nguyen
Srinivas Vasudev * Ugwu Leonard Ifeanyi, Jr.

Adolfo Pérez Esquivel ~ 1980

The Year of Peace
Celebrating past Nobel Peace Prize Recipients

The Poetry Posse 2020
Gail Weston Shazor * Albert Carasco * Hülya N. Yılmaz
Jackie Davis Allen * Caroline Nazareno * Eliza Segiet
Alicja Maria Kuberska * Teresa E. Gallion * Joe Paire
Kimberly Burnham * Shareef Abdur – Rasheed
Ashok K. Bhargava * Elizabeth Castillo * Swapna Behera
Tezmin Ition Tsai * William S. Peters, Sr.

Now Available
www.innerchildpress.com/the-year-of-the-poet

The Year of the Poet VII
September 2020

Featured Poets
Raed Anis Al-Jishi * Solkonvié Snezana
Dr. Brajesh Kumar Gupta * Umid Najjari

Mikhail Sergeyevich Gorbachev ~ 1990

The Year of Peace
Celebrating past Nobel Peace Prize Recipients

The Poetry Posse 2020
Gail Weston Shazor * Albert Carasco * Hülya N. Yılmaz
Jackie Davis Allen * Caroline Nazareno * Eliza Segiet
Alicja Maria Kuberska * Teresa E. Gallion * Joe Paire
Kimberly Burnham * Shareef Abdur ~ Rasheed
Ashok K. Bhargava * Elizabeth Castillo * Swapna Behera
Tezmin Ition Tsai * William S. Peters, Sr.

The Year of the Poet VII
October 2020

Featured Poets
Mutawaf A. Shaheed * Galina Italyanskaya
Nadeem Fraz * Avril Tanya Meallem

Kim Dae-jung ~ 2000

The Year of Peace
Celebrating past Nobel Peace Prize Recipients

The Poetry Posse 2020
Gail Weston Shazor * Albert Carasco * Hülya N. Yılmaz
Jackie Davis Allen * Caroline Nazareno * Eliza Segiet
Alicja Maria Kuberska * Teresa E. Gallion * Joe Paire
Kimberly Burnham * Shareef Abdur ~ Rasheed
Ashok K. Bhargava * Elizabeth Castillo * Swapna Behera
Tezmin Ition Tsai * William S. Peters, Sr.

The Year of the Poet VII
November 2020

Featured Poets
Elisa Mascia * Sue Lindenberg McClelland
Hatif Janabi * Ivan Gaćina

Liu Xiaobo ~ 2010

The Year of Peace
Celebrating past Nobel Peace Prize Recipients

The Poetry Posse 2020
Gail Weston Shazor * Albert Carasco * Hülya N. Yılmaz
Jackie Davis Allen * Caroline Nazareno * Eliza Segiet
Alicja Maria Kuberska * Teresa E. Gallion * Joe Paire
Kimberly Burnham * Shareef Abdur ~ Rasheed
Ashok K. Bhargava * Elizabeth Castillo * Swapna Behera
Tezmin Ition Tsai * William S. Peters, Sr.

The Year of the Poet VII
December 2020

Featured Poets
Ratan Ghosh * Ibtisam Ibrahim Al-Asady
Brindha Vinodh * Selma Kopic

Abiy Ahmed Ali ~ 2019

The Year of Peace
Celebrating past Nobel Peace Prize Recipients

The Poetry Posse 2020
Gail Weston Shazor * Albert Carasco * Hülya N. Yılmaz
Jackie Davis Allen * Caroline Nazareno * Eliza Segiet
Alicja Maria Kuberska * Teresa E. Gallion * Joe Paire
Kimberly Burnham * Shareef Abdur ~ Rasheed
Ashok K. Bhargava * Elizabeth Castillo * Swapna Behera
Tezmin Ition Tsai * William S. Peters, Sr.

Now Available
www.innerchildpress.com/the-year-of-the-poet

The Year of the Poet VIII
January 2021

Featured Global Poets
Andrew Scott * Debaprasanna Biswas
Shakil Kalam * Changming Yuan

Banksy's The Girl with the Pierced Eardrum

Poetry ... Ekphrasticly Speaking
The Poetry Posse 2020

Gail Weston Shazor * Albert Carasco * Hülya N. Yılmaz
Jackie Davis Allen * Caroline Nazareno * Eliza Segiet
Alicja Maria Kuberska * Teresa E. Gallion * Joe Paire
Kimberly Burnham * Shareef Abdur – Rasheed
Ashok K. Bhargava * Elizabeth Castillo * Swapna Behera
Tezmin Ition Tsai * William S. Peters, Sr.

The Year of the Poet VIII
February 2021

Featured Global Poets
T. Ramesh Babu * Ruchida Barman
Neptune Barman * Faleeha Hassan

Emory Douglas : 1968 Olympics mural

Poetry ... Ekphrasticly Speaking
The Poetry Posse 2021

Gail Weston Shazor * Albert Carasco * Hülya N. Yılmaz
Jackie Davis Allen * Caroline Nazareno * Eliza Segiet
Alicja Maria Kuberska * Teresa E. Gallion * Joe Paire
Kimberly Burnham * Shareef Abdur – Rasheed
Ashok K. Bhargava * Elizabeth Castillo * Swapna Behera
Tezmin Ition Tsai * William S. Peters, Sr.

The Year of the Poet VIII
March 2021

Featured Global Poets
Claudia Piccinno * Mohammed Jabr
Luzviminda Rivera * Nigar Arif

Tatyana Fazlalizadeh

Poetry ... Ekphrasticly Speaking
The Poetry Posse 2021

Gail Weston Shazor * Albert Carasco * Hülya N. Yılmaz
Jackie Davis Allen * Caroline Nazareno * Eliza Segiet
Alicja Maria Kuberska * Teresa E. Gallion * Joe Paire
Kimberly Burnham * Shareef Abdur – Rasheed
Ashok K. Bhargava * Elizabeth Castillo * Swapna Behera
Tezmin Ition Tsai * William S. Peters, Sr.

The Year of the Poet VIII
April 2021

Featured Global Poets
Katarzyna Brus- Sawczuk * Anwesha Paul
Rozalia Aleksandrova * Shahid Abbas

Pablo O'Higgins

Poetry ... Ekphrasticly Speaking
The Poetry Posse 2021

Gail Weston Shazor * Albert Carasco * Hülya N. Yılmaz
Jackie Davis Allen * Caroline Nazareno * Eliza Segiet
Alicja Maria Kuberska * Teresa E. Gallion * Joe Paire
Kimberly Burnham * Shareef Abdur – Rasheed
Ashok K. Bhargava * Elizabeth Castillo * Swapna Behera
Tezmin Ition Tsai * William S. Peters, Sr.

Now Available
www.innerchildpress.com/the-year-of-the-poet

The Year of the Poet VIII
May 2021

Featured Global Poets

Paramita Mukherjee Mullick * Rose Zerguine
Jaydeep Sarangi * Bismay Mohanty

Diego Rivera

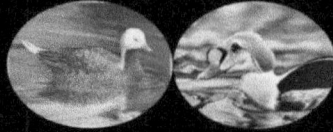

Poetry ... Ekphrasticly Speaking

The Poetry Posse 2021

Gail Weston Shazor * Albert Carasco * Hülya N. Yılmaz
Jackie Davis Allen * Caroline Nazareno * Eliza Segiet
Alicja Maria Kuberska * Teresa E. Gallion * Joe Paire
Kimberly Burnham * Shareef Abdur – Rasheed
Ashok K. Bhargava * Elizabeth Castillo * Swapna Behera
Tezmin Ition Tsai * William S. Peters, Sr.

The Year of the Poet VIII
June 2021

Featured Global Poets

Alonzo "zO" Gross * Lali Tsipi Michaeli
Tareq al Karmy * Tirthendu Ganguly

Rayen Kang

Poetry ... Ekphrasticly Speaking

The Poetry Posse 2021

Gail Weston Shazor * Albert Carasco * Hülya N. Yılmaz
Jackie Davis Allen * Caroline Nazareno * Eliza Segiet
Alicja Maria Kuberska * Teresa E. Gallion * Joe Paire
Kimberly Burnham * Shareef Abdur – Rasheed
Ashok K. Bhargava * Elizabeth Castillo * Swapna Behera
Tezmin Ition Tsai * William S. Peters, Sr.

The Year of the Poet VIII
July 2021

Featured Global Poets

Iram Jaan * Vesna Mundishevska-Veljanovska
Ngozi Olivia Osuoha * Lan Qyqalla

Goncalao Mabunda

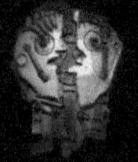

Poetry ... Ekphrasticly Speaking

The Poetry Posse 2021

Gail Weston Shazor * Albert Carasco * Hülya N. Yılmaz
Jackie Davis Allen * Caroline Nazareno * Eliza Segiet
Alicja Maria Kuberska * Teresa E. Gallion * Joe Paire
Kimberly Burnham * Shareef Abdur – Rasheed
Ashok K. Bhargava * Elizabeth Castillo * Swapna Behera
Tezmin Ition Tsai * William S. Peters, Sr.

The Year of the Poet VIII
August 2021

Featured Global Poets

Caroline Laurent Turunc * Kamal Dhungana
Pankhuri Sinha * Paramita Mukherjee Mullick

Mundara Koorang

Poetry ... Ekphrasticly Speaking

The Poetry Posse 2021

Gail Weston Shazor * Albert Carasco * Hülya N. Yılmaz
Jackie Davis Allen * Caroline Nazareno * Eliza Segiet
Alicja Maria Kuberska * Teresa E. Gallion * Joe Paire
Kimberly Burnham * Shareef Abdur – Rasheed
Ashok K. Bhargava * Elizabeth Castillo * Swapna Behera
Tezmin Ition Tsai * William S. Peters, Sr.

Now Available

www.innerchildpress.com/the-year-of-the-poet

The Year of the Poet VIII

September 2021

Featured Global Poets

Monsif Beroual * Sandesh Ghimire
Sharmila Poudel * Pavol Janik

Heather Jansch

Poetry . . . Ekphrasticly Speaking

The Poetry Posse 2021

Gail Weston Shazor * Albert Carasso * Hülya N. Yılmaz
Jackie Davis Allen * Caroline Nazareno * Eliza Segiet
Alicja Maria Kuberska * Teresa E. Gallion * Joe Paire
Kimberly Burnham * Shareef Abdur – Rasheed
Ashok K. Bhargava * Elizabeth Castillo * Swapna Behera
Tezmin Ition Tsai * William S. Peters, Sr.

The Year of the Poet VIII

October 2021

Featured Global Poets

C. E. Shy * Saswata Ganguly
Suranjit Gain * Hasiba Hilal

Dale Lamphere

Poetry . . . Ekphrasticly Speaking

The Poetry Posse 2021

Gail Weston Shazor * Albert Carasso * Hülya N. Yılmaz
Jackie Davis Allen * Caroline Nazareno * Eliza Segiet
Alicja Maria Kuberska * Teresa E. Gallion * Joe Paire
Kimberly Burnham * Shareef Abdur – Rasheed
Ashok K. Bhargava * Elizabeth Castillo * Swapna Behera
Tezmin Ition Tsai * William S. Peters, Sr.

The Year of the Poet VIII

November 2021

Featured Global Poets

Errol D. Bean * Ibrahim Honjo
Tanja Ajtic * Rajashree Mohapatra

Andy Goldsworthy

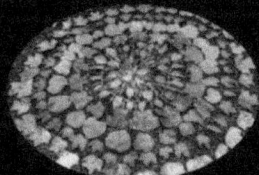

Poetry . . . Ekphrasticly Speaking

The Poetry Posse 2021

Gail Weston Shazor * Albert Carasso * Hülya N. Yılmaz
Jackie Davis Allen * Caroline Nazareno * Eliza Segiet
Alicja Maria Kuberska * Teresa E. Gallion * Joe Paire
Kimberly Burnham * Shareef Abdur – Rasheed
Ashok K. Bhargava * Elizabeth Castillo * Swapna Behera
Tezmin Ition Tsai * William S. Peters, Sr.

The Year of the Poet VIII

December 2021

Featured Global Poets

Orbinda Ganga * Fadairo Tesleem
Anthony Arnold * Iyad Shamasnah

Fredric Edwin Church

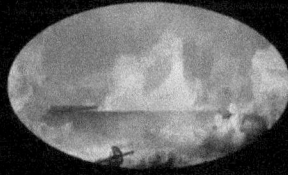

Poetry . . . Ekphrasticly Speaking

The Poetry Posse 2021

Gail Weston Shazor * Albert Carasso * Hülya N. Yılmaz
Jackie Davis Allen * Caroline Nazareno * Eliza Segiet
Alicja Maria Kuberska * Teresa E. Gallion * Joe Paire
Kimberly Burnham * Shareef Abdur – Rasheed
Ashok K. Bhargava * Elizabeth Castillo * Swapna Behera
Tezmin Ition Tsai * William S. Peters, Sr.

Now Available

www.innerchildpress.com/the-year-of-the-poet

The Year of the Poet IX

January 2022

Featured Global Poets

**Ratan Ghosh * Christine Neil-Wright
Andrew Scott * Ashok Kumar**

Climate Change : The Ice Cap

Poetry . . . Ekphrasticly Speaking

The Poetry Posse 2021

Gail Weston Shazor * Albert Carasco * Hülya N. Yılmaz
Jackie Davis Allen * Caroline Nazareno * Eliza Segiet
Alicja Maria Kuberska * Teresa E. Gallion * Joe Paire
Kimberly Burnham * Shareef Abdur – Rasheed
Ashok K. Bhargava * Elizabeth Castillo * Swapna Behera
Tezmin Ition Tsai * William S. Peters, Sr.

The Year of the Poet IX

February 2022

Featured Global Poets

Roza Boyanova * Ramón de Jesús Núñez Duval
Mammad Ismayil * Tarana Turan Rahimli

Climate Change and Mountains

Poetry . . . Ekphrasticly Speaking

The Poetry Posse 2021

Gail Weston Shazor * Albert Carasco * Hülya N. Yılmaz
Jackie Davis Allen * Caroline Nazareno * Eliza Segiet
Alicja Maria Kuberska * Teresa E. Gallion * Joe Paire
Kimberly Burnham * Shareef Abdur – Rasheed
Ashok K. Bhargava * Elizabeth Castillo * Swapna Behera
Tezmin Ition Tsai * William S. Peters, Sr.

The Year of the Poet IX

March 2022

Featured Global Poets

Dimitris P. Kraniotis * Marlene Pasini
Kennedy Ochieng * Swayam Prashant

Climate Change and Space Debris

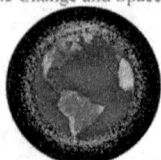

Poetry . . . Ekphrasticly Speaking

The Poetry Posse 2021

Gail Weston Shazor * Albert Carasco * Hülya N. Yılmaz
Jackie Davis Allen * Caroline Nazareno * Eliza Segiet
Alicja Maria Kuberska * Teresa E. Gallion * Joe Paire
Kimberly Burnham * Shareef Abdur – Rasheed
Ashok K. Bhargava * Elizabeth Castillo * Swapna Behera
Tezmin Ition Tsai * William S. Peters, Sr.

The Year of the Poet IX

April 2022

Featured Global Poets

**Alonzo Gross * Dr. Debaprasanna Biswas
Monsif Beroual * Carol Aronoff**

Climate Change and Oceans

*Celebrating our 100th Edition *

Poetry . . . Ekphrasticly Speaking

The Poetry Posse 2021

Gail Weston Shazor * Albert Carasco * Hülya N. Yılmaz
Jackie Davis Allen * Caroline Nazareno * Eliza Segiet
Alicja Maria Kuberska * Teresa E. Gallion * Joe Paire
Kimberly Burnham * Shareef Abdur – Rasheed
Ashok K. Bhargava * Elizabeth Castillo * Swapna Behera
Tezmin Ition Tsai * William S. Peters, Sr.

Now Available

www.innerchildpress.com/the-year-of-the-poet

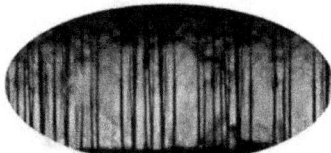

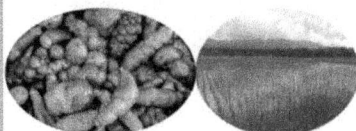

The Year of the Poet IX
September 2022

Featured Global Poets

Ngozi Olivia Osuoha * Biswajit Mishra
Sylwia K. Malinowska * Sajid Hussein

Climate Change and Wind and Weather Patterns

Poetry ... Ekphrasticly Speaking

The Poetry Posse 2022

Gail Weston Shazor * Albert Carasco * Hülya N. Yılmaz
Jackie Davis Allen * Caroline Nazareno * Eliza Segiet
Alicja Maria Kubeska * Teresa E. Gallion * Joe Paire
Kimberly Burnham * Shareef Abdur – Rasheed
Ashok K. Bhargava * Elizabeth Castillo * Swapna Behera
Tezmin Ition Tsai * William S. Peters, Sr.

The Year of the Poet IX
October 2022

Featured Global Poets

Andrew Kouroupos * Brenda Mohammed
Carthornia Kouroupos * Faleeha Hassan

Climate Change and Oil and Power

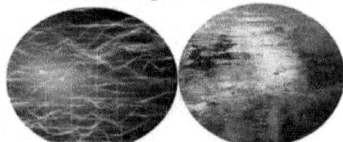

Poetry ... Ekphrasticly Speaking

The Poetry Posse 2022

Gail Weston Shazor * Albert Carasco * Hülya N. Yılmaz
Jackie Davis Allen * Caroline Nazareno * Eliza Segiet
Alicja Maria Kubeska * Teresa E. Gallion * Joe Paire
Kimberly Burnham * Shareef Abdur – Rasheed
Ashok K. Bhargava * Elizabeth Castillo * Swapna Behera
Tezmin Ition Tsai * William S. Peters, Sr.

The Year of the Poet IX
November 2022

Featured Global Poets

Hema Ravi * Shafkat Aziz Hajam
Selma Kopic * Ibrahim Honjo

Climate Change : Time to Act

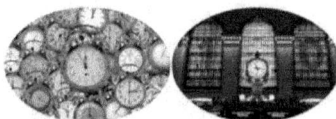

Poetry ... Ekphrasticly Speaking

The Poetry Posse 2022

Gail Weston Shazor * Albert Carasco * Hülya N. Yılmaz
Jackie Davis Allen * Caroline Nazareno * Eliza Segiet
Alicja Maria Kubeska * Teresa E. Gallion * Joe Paire
Kimberly Burnham * Shareef Abdur – Rasheed
Ashok K. Bhargava * Elizabeth Castillo * Swapna Behera
Tezmin Ition Tsai * William S. Peters, Sr.

The Year of the Poet IX
December 2022

Featured Global Poets

Elarbi Abdelfattah * Lorraine Cragg
Neha Bhandarkar * Robert Gibbons

Climate Change Bees, Butterflies and Insect Life

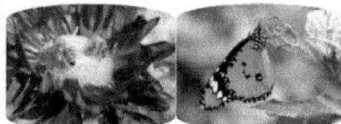

Poetry ... Ekphrasticly Speaking

The Poetry Posse 2022

Gail Weston Shazor * Albert Carasco * Hülya N. Yılmaz
Jackie Davis Allen * Caroline Nazareno * Eliza Seigiet
Alicja Maria Kubeska * Teresa E. Gallion * Joe Paire
Kimberly Burnham * Shareef Abdur – Rasheed
Ashok K. Bhargava * Elizabeth Castillo * Swapna Behera
Tezmin Ition Tsai * William S. Peters, Sr.

Now Available

www.innerchildpress.com/the-year-of-the-poet

The Year of the Poet X
January 2023

Featured Global Poets

JuNe Barefield * Swayam Prashant
Willow Rose * Shabbirhusein K Jamnagerwalla

Children : Difference Makers

Iqbal Masih

The Poetry Posse 2023

Gail Weston Shazor * Albert Carasco * Hülya N. Yılmaz
Jackie Davis Allen * Caroline Nazareno * Kimberly Burnham
Alicja Maria Kuberska * Teresa E. Gallion * Joe Paire
Michelle Joan Barulich * Shareef Abdur – Rasheed
Ashok K. Bhargava * Elizabeth Castillo * Swapna Behera
Tezmin Ition Tsai * Eliza Segiet * William S. Peters, Sr.

The Year of the Poet X
February 2023

Featured Global Poets

Christena Williams * Hilda Graciela Kraft
Francesco Favetta * Dr. H.C. Louise Hudon

Children : Difference Makers

Ruby Bridges

The Poetry Posse 2023

Gail Weston Shazor * Albert Carasco * Hülya N. Yılmaz
Jackie Davis Allen * Caroline Nazareno * Kimberly Burnham
Alicja Maria Kuberska * Teresa E. Gallion * Joe Paire
Michelle Joan Barulich * Shareef Abdur – Rasheed
Ashok K. Bhargava * Elizabeth Castillo * Swapna Behera
Tezmin Ition Tsai * Eliza Segiet * William S. Peters, Sr.

The Year of the Poet X
March 2023

Featured Global Poets

Clarena Martínez Turizo * Binod Dawadi
Til Kumari Sharma * Petrouchka Alexieva

Children : Difference Makers

Yo Yo Ma

The Poetry Posse 2023

Gail Weston Shazor * Albert Carasco * Hülya N. Yılmaz
Jackie Davis Allen * Caroline Nazareno * Kimberly Burnham
Alicja Maria Kuberska * Teresa E. Gallion * Joe Paire
Michelle Joan Barulich * Shareef Abdur – Rasheed
Ashok K. Bhargava * Elizabeth Castillo * Swapna Behera
Tezmin Ition Tsai * Eliza Segiet * William S. Peters, Sr.

The Year of the Poet X
April 2023

Featured Global Poets

Maxwanette A Poetess * Alonzo Gross
Türkan Ergör. * Ibrahim Honjo

Children : Difference Makers

Claudette Colvin

The Poetry Posse 2023

Gail Weston Shazor * Albert Carasco * Hülya N. Yılmaz
Jackie Davis Allen * Caroline Nazareno * Kimberly Burnham
Alicja Maria Kuberska * Teresa E. Gallion * Joe Paire
Michelle Joan Barulich * Shareef Abdur – Rasheed
Ashok K. Bhargava * Elizabeth Castillo * Swapna Behera
Tezmin Ition Tsai * Eliza Segiet * William S. Peters, Sr.

Now Available

www.innerchildpress.com/the-year-of-the-poet

The Year of the Poet X
May 2023

Csp Shrivastava * Michael Lee Johnson
Taghrid Bou Merhi * Yasmin Brown
Children : Difference Makers

Louis Braille
The Poetry Posse 2023

Gail Weston Shazor * Albert Carasco * Hülya N. Yılmaz
Jackie Davis Allen * Caroline Nazareno * Kimberly Burnham
Alicja Maria Kuberska * Teresa E. Gallion * Joe Paire
Michelle Joan Barulich * Shareef Abdur – Rasheed
Ashok K. Bhargava * Elizabeth Castillo * Swapna Behera
Tezmin Ition Tsai * Eliza Segiet * William S. Peters, Sr.

The Year of the Poet X
June 2023

Featured Global Poets
Kay Peters · Carthornia Kouroupos
Andrew Kouroupos · Faleeha Hassan
Children : Difference Makers

Ryan Hreljac
The Poetry Posse 2023

The Year of the Poet X
July 2023

Featured Global Poets
Rajashree Mohapatra * Biswajit Mishra
Johan Karlsson * Teodozja Świderska

Children : Difference Makers

~ Bana al-Abed ~
The Poetry Posse 2023

Gail Weston Shazor * Albert Carasco * Hülya N. Yılmaz
Jackie Davis Allen * Caroline Nazareno * Kimberly Burnham
Alicja Maria Kuberska * Teresa E. Gallion * Joe Paire
Michelle Joan Barulich * Shareef Abdur – Rasheed
Ashok K. Bhargava * Elizabeth Castillo * Swapna Behera
Tezmin Ition Tsai * Eliza Segiet * William S. Peters, Sr.

The Year of the Poet X
August 2023

Featured Global Poets
Kennedy Wanda Ochieng * Jose Lopez
Sylwia K. Malinowska * Laurent Grison

Children : Difference Makers

~ Kelvin Doe ~
The Poetry Posse 2023

Gail Weston Shazor * Albert Carasco * Hülya N. Yılmaz
Jackie Davis Allen * Caroline Nazareno * Kimberly Burnham
Alicja Maria Kuberska * Teresa E. Gallion * Joe Paire
Michelle Joan Barulich * Shareef Abdur – Rasheed
Ashok K. Bhargava * Elizabeth Castillo * Swapna Behera
Tezmin Ition Tsai * Eliza Segiet * William S. Peters, Sr.

Now Available
www.innerchildpress.com/the-year-of-the-poet

and there is much, much more !

visit . . .

www.innerchildpress.com/antho
logies-sales-special.php

Also check out our Authors and
all the wonderful Books
Available at :

www.innerchildpress.com/autho
rs-pages

Coming Soon

From

Inner Child Press International

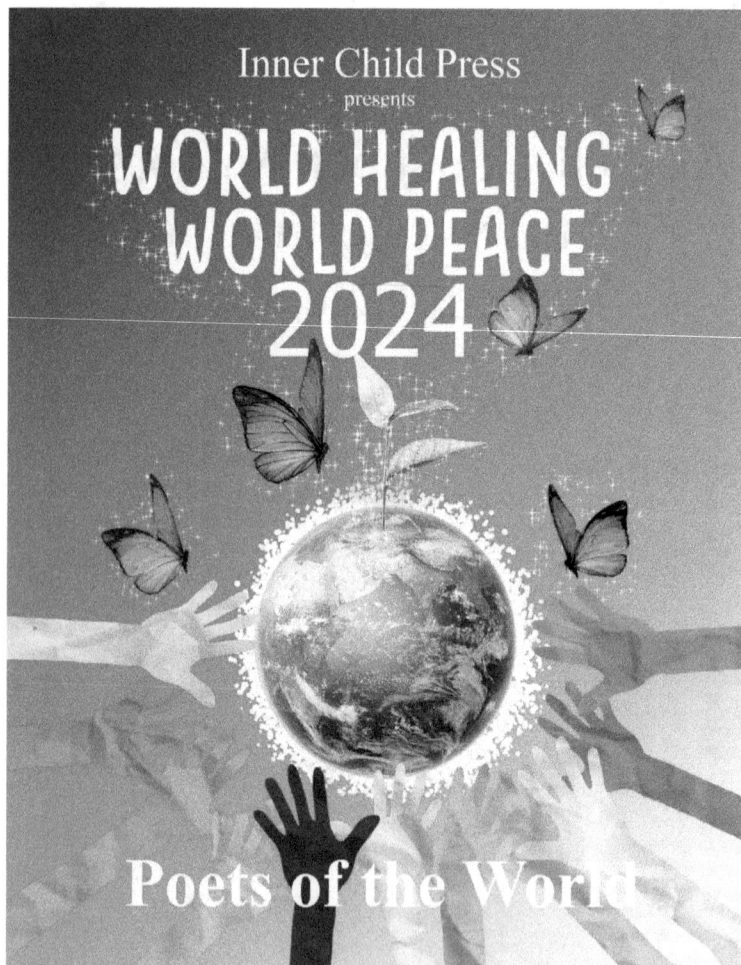

Inner Child Press
presents

WORLD HEALING
WORLD PEACE
2024

Poets of the World

Letter Poems

to our

Deceased

featuring

Poets of the World

INNER CHILD PRESS

BLACK
MALE~d

a collaboration of BLACKNESS

Volume II

The Black Male ~ d Writers

World Healing World Peace
2020

Poets for Humanity

Now Available

www.worldhealingworldpeacepoetry.com

INNER CHILD PRESS

WORLD HEALING
WORLD PEACE
2018

A Poetry Anthology for Humanity

Now Available

www.worldhealingworldpeacepoetry.com

i support

World Healing
World Peace

www.worldhealingworldpeacepoetry.com

241

World Healing
World Peace
2012, 2014, 2016, 2018, 2020, 2022

Now Available

www.worldhealingworldpeacepoetry.com

Inner Child Press International
'building bridges of cultural understanding'
Meet our Cultural Ambassadors

Fahredin Shehu
Director of Cultural

Falcha Hassan
Iraq - USA

Elizabeth E. Castillo
Philippines

Antoinette Coleman
Chicago
Midwest USA

Ananda Nepali
Nepal - Tibet
Northern India

Kimberly Burnham
Pacific Northwest
USA

Alicja Kuberska
Poland
Eastern Europe

Swapna Behera
India
Southeast Asia

Kolade O. Freedom
Nigeria
West Africa

Moustf Beroual
Morocco
Northern Africa

Ashok K. Bhargava
Canada

Tzemin Ition Tsai
Republic of China
Greater China

Alicia M. Ramirez
Mexico
Central America

Christena AV Williams
Jamaica
Caribbean

Louise Hudon
Eastern Canada

Aziz Mountassir
Morocco
Northern Africa

Shareef Abdur-Rasheed
Southeastern USA

Laure Charazac
France
Western Europe

Mohammad Ikbal Harb
Lebanon
Middle East

Mohamed Abdel
Aziz Shmeis
Egypt
Middle East

Hilary Mainga
Kenya
United Africa

Josephus R. Johnson
Liberia

www.innerchildpress.com

This Anthological Publication
is underwritten solely by

Inner Child Press International

Inner Child Press is a Publishing Company
Founded and Operated by Writers. Our
personal publishing experiences provides
us an intimate understanding of the
sometimes daunting challenges Writers,
New and Seasoned may face in the
Business of Publishing and Marketing
their Creative "Written Work".

For more Information

Inner Child Press International

www.innerchildpress.com

building bridges of cultural understanding
www.innerchildpress.com
202 Wiltree Court, State College, Pennsylvania 16801

~ fini ~

www.ingramcontent.com/pod-product-compliance
Lightning Source LLC
LaVergne TN
LVHW022321080426
835508LV00041B/1659